SOCIAL INTERACTION AS DRAMA

To June Sara Rabson Hare, who introduced me
to the dramaturgical perspective
through psychodrama
and her own special
dramatic talents

SOCIAL INTERACTION AS DRAMA

Applications from Conflict Resolution

A. PAUL HARE

SAGE PUBLICATIONS
Beverly Hills   London   New Delhi

Copyright © 1985 by Sage Publications, Inc.

For information address:

SAGE Publications, Inc.
275 South Beverly Drive
Beverly Hills, California 90212

SAGE Publications India Pvt. Ltd.
M-32 Market
Greater Kailash I
New Delhi 110 048 India

SAGE Publications Ltd
28 Banner Street
London EC1Y 8QE
England

Printed in the United States of America

Library of Congress Cataloging in Publication Data

Hare, A. Paul (Alexander Paul), 1923-
    Social interaction as drama.

    Bibliography: p. 171
    Includes index.
    1. Social interaction.   2. Role playing.
3. Symbolic interactionism.   4. Social conflict—
Case studies.   5. Conflict management—Case studies.
I. Title
HM136.H28   1985   302   84-26275
ISBN 0-8039-2429-1
ISBN 0-8039-2430-5 (pbk.)

FIRST PRINTING

Contents

Preface

The basic assumption for the analysis of social interaction as drama is that meaningful interaction takes place between individuals when they enact roles in support of some idea. In keeping with this assumption, this book may be considered as an opening monologue delivered to you, the reader, as audience. Depending upon your own familiarity with this dramaturgical perspective and the particular instances of conflict and conflict resolution that will be used to illustrate the application of the perspective, you may wish to adopt one or more of the following roles as a counter-player in support of this idea. If you are unfamiliar with the dramaturgical perspective in social psychology, then it is my hope that this book will serve as a fair introduction to it and that you will be encouraged to read further in this area. If you are already familiar with the dramaturgical perspective as it exists in the current literature, you will be aware that I have extended the perspective by adding insights from the study of interaction process and of functional analysis in groups as well as from the writings of persons associated with the theater. I hope you will be encouraged to expand the perspective still further. If your main interest is in conflict or conflict resolution involving labor disputes, protests, riots, or ethnic disputes involving parts of nations or whole nations, then I hope that you will find this perspective useful for analysis and intervention.

The dramaturgical perspective in social psychology was developed mainly by persons working in the symbolic interactionist tradition of the "Chicago School." The broader symbolic interactionist theory gave considerable attention to the process of socialization of children as they acquired roles, whereas the persons who analyzed social interaction as drama were concerned with adult role players.

The theory presented here views all social interaction as a form of drama, with creativity at the heart of the matter. For this theory, the

7

literature on theater, including books written by actors and directors, provides a set of insights about the nature of human interaction. Over the years playwrights, directors, and actors have specialized in a process that is central to collective behavior: the communication of an idea to an audience. In everyday life there may be only two people present or there may be many, but the initial problem is the same. Before there can be any collective behavior, one actor must transmit an idea to another actor or to an audience. A major difference between everyday life and the theater is that an ordinary person continually modifies the presentation of the idea in response to the reactions of the listener, whereas the actor follows a fixed script until the play is finished.

In everyday life, as people react to an idea either positively, negatively, or indifferently, some are moved to take roles in support of the idea, others to take roles that are critical of the idea, and some to remain neutral. If the idea that is presented is not the espouser's own, there may be someone similar to a playwright behind the scenes who created the idea. There may also be someone who facilitates the presentation of the idea like a director. There is always a stage, or action area, where the activity takes place. Persons who are outside this action space form the audience. The time during which a presentation takes place is always limited. It may be only a few minutes or it may be a lifetime; an actor, however, cannot hold the stage forever.

In groups of different types, activity is organized differently. In the small informal group, activity is often organized around an "image," an object, an action, or a word picture that provides an emotionally loaded focus of attention. In larger informal groups, such as street crowds, the activity may follow a "theme" that provides a general direction and mood of action. For social movements, the organizing ideas are more complicated, as in a "plot," where phases of the activity over time are outlined with an indication of the major roles to be played and the nature of the group's objective for interaction in an organization, such as a factory or a university, the central idea takes the form of a "script" in which specific tasks are described and the details of roles are given.

In many groups, several images, themes, plots, or scripts are being enacted at the same time, some formally and others informally. Sometimes the presentation is enacted by the same actors and at other times by different actors who take over the action space in turn. Thus life can be seen as "ever changing, ever renewing drama" (Sarbin, in Allen and Scheibe, 1982: 33).

These are the basic ideas to be expanded in the text. However, before going on to outline the contents of this volume, I would like to provide the reader with a brief description of some parts of my own background that led to the choice of this perspective and field of application.

This book provides an opportunity for me to bring together two themes that have characterized my own activities from childhood. One has to do with the theater and various forms of entertainment and the other with conflict resolution. Although on many occasions I played a supporting role, I remember best the ones that I helped to organize. I always enjoyed doing things a little differently. One of my early heroes was Henry David Thoreau who said that he "marched to the beat of a different drummer" (Thoreau, 1949: 216). In my own case, because I started playing drums with a drum and bugle corps in junior high school, I was often the "different drummer."

Without going into all the details, I remember that my first 25 years—whether in school, Boy Scouts, college, or the U.S. Army—I usually acted as the social director, organizing skits, plays, or fun and games. Because I was a cartoonist and made posters to advertise the events, I had ample opportunity to capture the "image" of social events on a two-dimensional page. For several seasons when I was still in High School, I accompanied my mother to all Saturday matinees at the National Theater in Washington, D.C. As an English major at Swarthmore College, I read classic and modern plays and attended the local repertory theater, as well as theaters in Philadelphia and New York whenever possible.

Sociology was not taught at Swarthmore when I was there, so it was not until I moved on to Iowa State University (Ames) to study architectural engineering that I took a required course in sociology. Here I found people professionally concerned with groups, whereas I had only been an amateur. I decided to drop architecture and give up my position as a teaching assistant in physics (although not my interest in the experimental method) and concentrate on sociology. By taking a double load of courses, I was able to complete a second Bachelor's Degree in one year and move on to graduate work in sociology and social psychology, first at the University of Pennsylvania and then at the University of Chicago where I became immersed in the "social interactionist" tradition.

I had the good fortune to be around Harvard University in the heyday of small group research (from the mid-1950s to 1960), first in the School of Public Health and then in Social Relations as one of Freed

Bales's assistants. Thus I became thoroughly familiar with Bales's systems for observing groups, which culminated in the multilevel observation system that he uses now. It was only after I left Harvard for Haverford College in 1960 that I became acquainted with Parsonian functional analysis through the good offices of my colleague Andrew Effrat.

My interest in conflict resolution can also be traced back to my early childhood when I was more likely to be "holding the coats" of the antagonists rather than directly involved on one side of a conflict. However it was not until after World War II that I joined others, especially Quakers, who were concerned that the civil rights of all Americans were not yet in accord with statements in the Constitution. At Harvard I initiated and became co-chairman of the Fair Housing Committee of Weston, Massachusetts, one of many committees concerned with opening white Anglo-Saxon Christian suburbs to persons of other ethnic or religious backgrounds. Similarly, at Haverford College I initiated and became co-chairman of the Radnor Township Fair Housing Committee and later the Ardmore Coalition, both devoted to goals similar to those I had tried to address in Weston.

During 1961-1962 I had the opportunity to serve as the Deputy Representative of the Peace Corps in the Philippines. Although there was not much emphasis on peace in the Peace Corps, we did try responding to the needs of rural people by introducing new ideas in the schools and in the communities. The Peace Corps experience gave me the confidence to organize a group of academics and community workers committed to nonviolence to help the people of Curacao, Netherlands Antilles, come together to discuss common problems after a riot in 1969 that brought down the government. Our third-party intervention took the form of the 1970 summer Antillian Institute of Social Science, of which I was co-director.

In the mid-1960s I established the Center for Nonviolent Conflict Resolution at Haverford College. Our involvement with the peace movement led to a major grant from the National Institute of Mental Health to observe the various forms of nonviolent protest in Washington, D.C., and in other parts of America during the late 1960s and early 1970s. This in turn led to my taking part in a group of faculty and students acting as third parties at Kent State University during the academic year 1970-1971 following a protest the previous spring during which four students had been killed. We were engaged in a variety of nonviolent activities designed to prevent the reoccurrence of the previous violent confrontation. A second outcome of the

Haverford Center activity was that I was asked by members of the
International Peace Academy staff to help organize a group of volunteers to serve as third-party mediators on Cyprus (1972-1974) to
help bring the Greek and Turkish communities closer together. Some
of the details of this project are found in Chapter 4 of this volume. To
recruit volunteers for the Cyprus project and on several other occasions, I had the opportunity to observe, and in some cases participate
in, the work of the Gandhian Shanti Sena (Peace Brigade) in India in
relief, community development, and riot control. Case studies of
some of the major nonviolent actions in America and other parts of
the world were collected in the volumes that I edited together with
Herbert Blumberg entitled *Nonviolent Direct Action: American
Cases: Social-Psychological Analyses* (1968), *Liberation Without*
Violence: A Third Party Approach (1977), and *A Search for Peace
and Justice: Reflections of Michael Scott* (1980).

   After moving to the University of Cape Town, South Africa in
1973, I became involved as a third party in confrontations between
black people and the white government, especially in the so-called
Coloured schools in the Cape Town area. In 1976 at the time of a major
period of unrest, I helped form and I served as coordinator for a
voluntary ambulance unit to help with medical transportation in the
black squatters' areas and to provide emergency and third-party
service at times of confrontations between police and community
members. The ambulance service was again visible during the 1980
period of unrest (see the description of the incident at Elsies River in
Chapter 3). The ambulance unit also provided a model of the type of
service that might be performed by conscientious objectors, should
the government decide to accept some national civilian service as an
alternative to prison. Some indication of the parts played by those of
us concerned with nonviolent action and conflict resolution during
those years is reflected in the case material in *The Struggle for
Democracy in South Africa: Conflict and Conflict Resolution* (Hare,
1983b).

   In 1980 I moved to Ben-Gurion University in Israel, and then
returned to Cape Town in 1981 to complete my teaching commitment
and to bring together my experience with conflict and conflict resolution in the volume noted above. Until now I have been occupied
mainly with the problems of settling in to a new country and living and
working on a kibbutz as a resident for one year. In India, the followers
of Gandhi are sometimes involved in protest, sometimes in conflict
resolution, sometimes in social change, and sometimes in living

together in community. They believe that all of these activities are necessary parts of the search for truth. Rather than spending time deciding where to place the emphasis in their activities, they say "do what comes before you." So I shall see what opportunities are placed before me in the years to come and how they can be creatively experienced.

Now back to the formal part of the preface. You will find that the book is presented in two parts. Part I introduces the dramaturgical perspective from social-psychology and brings together some of the insights provided by persons working in the theater. Part II consists of applications of the dramaturgical perspective in the analysis of instances of conflict involving protest and instances of conflict resolution between ethnic and national groups. I was involved in only two of the instances described in Part II as a participant rather than as an observer. Even then the events took place before I had begun to use the dramaturgical perspective as it is presented here. As a result only one or two aspects of each case have been highlighted as illustrations of the type of analysis that can be made in the future when more formal methods of observation are used at the time the event occurs. The final section of the book consists of three appendices for readers who wish more details about dramatism in social psychology, phase movement in collective behavior, and types of dramatic situations.

A. Paul Hare

Acknowledgments

First I wish to thank those publishers who have allowed me to reprint selected material of my own and of others. Specific acknowledgments are given at the points in the text where the quotations appear.

Second, I am most grateful to those colleagues who read this manuscript at various stages of preparation. They have helped change the presentation from a monologue to more of a dialogue; at least I have tried to be more responsive to the kinds of questions that they raised and that other readers might also raise. Thanks to Sol Levine, Paul Shane, David Naveh, Alex Weingrod, and to my wife, June Rabson Hare.

PART I

SOCIAL INTERACTION AS DRAMA

Life is ever changing, ever renewing drama.
—Theodore Sarbin, 1982

Chapter 1

A Word on Plays

Many theories of social psychology have as a basic assumption that social interaction is organized around some idea. Some of these ideas have a narrow focus such as the stereotype of another person or group or the attribution of causality to a particular person or event. Some of the ideas cover a broader area such as the expectations concerning the roles to be played in a given situation. As the social interaction is played out over time, it takes place in a series of episodes that may build to a climax followed by a resolution, much as the development of a play as it is enacted in the theater.

As an introduction to a dramaturgical perspective on social interaction, four sets of concepts are presented. First a suggestion about the range of ideas around which social interaction is organized, second a basic list of roles and aspects of the situation that influence the development of the ideas, third an indication of the elements of form, process, and content of social interaction that should be considered when describing its dramatic development, and fourth an indication of the ways that roles might be combined in an organization or network and in a small group.

Many concepts and hypotheses are packed into this first chapter. The social-psychological perspective that will be introduced here takes as its starting point terms that have been used in dramatic or psychodramatic performances; however, the chapter is not limited to these ideas. Rather the ultimate goal is to include all relevant aspects of social-psychological theory. Some of the similarities between

AUTHOR'S NOTE: This chapter is based primarily on a paper presented at the meeting of the American Sociological Society in San Antonio, August, 1984 and a report to the Human Sciences Research Council of South Africa submitted in 1983.

performances in the theater and in everyday life have already been suggested in the preface to this volume and are elaborated on further in Chapter 2 and in Appendix I.

Ideas

The ideas that provide a focus for social interaction can be placed along a continuum from those that are relatively simple to those that are complex and provide detailed prescriptions for the roles to be played. "Image," "theme," "plot," and "script" are four points along this continuum. An *image* can be a set of words or a physical object or an event that is emotionally loaded—for example, "ghetto," "blood bath," "bacchanalia," "May Day" (Bales and Cohen, 1979: 32).[1] Images are more likely to guide interaction in informal groups or therapy groups where there is relatively little role differentiation and the "work" of the group is not rigidly defined. In groups of this type, once an image is presented, members tend to take sides, some being for and some being against the image. Within each subgroup, the persons for whom the image is especially relevant will become leaders. If the positive and negative split is marked, the group may become polarized. On the next round a new image may unify the group.

A *theme* suggests some movement over time. It includes both a direction of movement and a minimal set of roles to be enacted. Interaction organized around a theme is most likely to be found in collective behavior, the "emergent and extra-institutional social forms and behavior" seen in panic-stricken, riotous, and ecstatic crowds (Lofland, 1981). The term *plot* is used to suggest a more detailed scenario with more definition of the roles to be followed and the stages the group must go through in order to reach the goal. Social movements, in which people come together to do something about their common concern have this initial character (Zurcher and Snow, 1981). The most complete set of directions for social behavior are presented in the form of *scripts* where the interaction of each of the actors is specified as the play develops through a series of acts. The behavior of persons in organizations takes this form (Katz and Kahn, 1978).[2]

The ideas that are presented at the image end of the continuum tend to reflect and depend upon the characters or personalities of the actors; whereas those at the script end of the continuum provide formats for social interaction with little regard for the personalities of the persons who are enacting the roles. This distinction between the two ends of the continuum is similar to the description of "character driven" versus "plot driven" dramas that will be developed in Chapter 2.

Roles and the Situation

Within social psychology the "symbolic interactionist" approach has always focused on the concept of "role," that is, on a set of activities that are expected of a person who fills a given position in a group (Stryker, 1981; see Appendix 1). Cooley (1902) and Mead (1934), who were carriers for this tradition at the University of Chicago, observed that children are socialized by learning to take roles. A role is learned as part of a set of roles that have mutual obligations in the form of rights and duties, or more generally, "expectations." For Mead, the child passed through three iden- tifiable stages in learning roles; first informal play, then more formal games, and finally taking the role of the "generalized other" as a perspective on his or her own enactments and those of other actors in the situation. Thomas indicated that the actors would choose their roles in response to their "definition of the situation" (Volkart, 1951). In terms of dramaturgical theory, the "definition of the situation" is essentially a statement about the idea around which the interaction is to develop.[3] In most situations, several distinct roles are required to allow a set of persons to respond adequately to the requirements of the situation.[4]

With rare exceptions, such as when Buber (1970) or Sartre (Caws, 1979) manage to cast aside most of the everyday requirements of roles and act on a self-to-self basis, the social behavior we observe is actually "role enactment" (Sarbin, in Allen and Scheibe, 1982: 38). However in social psychology the connection between the roles that are played and the ideas around which they are organized has not been made explicit in much of the literature. Usually persons who study organizations discuss roles but do not mention the organizing ideas, other than to state the general purpose of the organization. On the other hand, persons who study collective behavior are quite concerned with the ideas but do not say very much about the various roles being played within the subgroups of the larger collectivity.

Even Bales and Cohen (1979), who give one of the most complete discussions of how images affect behavior in small groups, cite the concept "role" only six times in the index of their book, mainly with reference to a summary statement about an individual's behavior rather than to a set of expectations.[5]

Basic Roles

Because all behavior in a given situation is essentially behavior in role, it is useful to have a set of generalized roles that one can look for when observing social interaction. For a start, we turn to Moreno who developed the therapeutic method of "psychodrama" from his observations of the therapeutic effects of persons playing roles in the theater. His set of four basic roles in a psychodrama can be used for analysis in other situations (Moreno, 1953):

(1)   A *director* who organizes the activity and may or may not be present at the time the group is observed.

(2)   One or more *protagonists* who present images, themes, plots, or scripts that guide group activity or whose role is central for the illusion in the play. If a role is in opposition to one of the protagonists, the person is an *antagonist*.

(3)   *Auxiliaries*, persons who play roles supporting the protagonists.

(4)   Members of the *audience* whose response verifies the meaning of the activity and who in turn may become protagonists on another occasion.

Two additional roles from the theater can be added that do not usually appear in a psychodrama:[6]

(5)   A *playwright* who develops the image, theme, plot, or script, but does not appear on stage to enact it.

(6)   Members of a *chorus*, a group of auxiliaries who act in unison to concentrate the emotions of the audience on particular moods or attention on particular events, or help interpret them in a certain way.

A more detailed description of each of these roles that draws on material provided by persons involved with theater is given in Chapter 2. In addition a list of techniques is presented, based on those used in psychodrama, that protagonists or auxiliaries may employ in presenting their ideas. An indication of the sets of roles that occur most often in the theater and in everyday life is also provided.

To the basic list of roles we add two important aspects of the situation. One is the *stage* and its setting that place broad limits on the kind of activity that can be developed (Burke, 1968: 446). Persons also behave differently onstage, offstage, and backstage (Goffman, 1959: 106-140). The other aspect of the situation is the *time* available (Bales and Cohen, 1979: 66). The pressure to complete an activity in limited time is the most common form of stress for a group.

Elements of Social Interaction

Up to this point we have focused on the ideas and the roles that enact them as essential features of the dramaturgical perspective. However, our goal is to understand social interaction. The elements of social interaction are given in Figure 1.1. Social interaction has three aspects: form, process, and content (Hare, 1982: 20-22). Because the social behavior of any individual represents some compromise between the expectations of role and the tendencies of personality, the task of predicting interaction from measures of personality and role becomes simpler if the same aspects are identified in all three systems. In Figure 1.1, the three aspects are given as they would be used to describe interaction.

The two variables involved in the *form* of interaction are more easily recorded than either the process or the content. These variables are the communication network and the interaction rate. That is, one can observe which persons are connected by communication channels and how much communication passes along each channel.

For the analysis of *process* in a group, the most frequent division is between process primarily directed toward the solution of task problems and process primarily directed towards the solution of social-emotional problems. Many category systems, such as those of Bales (1950) and Bion (1961), include both types of process, whereas others concentrate on only one area. Within the task area, the minimum set of categories would parallel the steps in the scientific method, namely: observation, hypothesis formation, and the testing of hypotheses. For dramaturgical analysis it is helpful to identify the level of creativity involved (Hare, 1982: 45). The categories given in Figure 1.1 for the process of Task Behavior represent a continuum from actions that are self-oriented and unrelated to group work to those actions that are highly creative in that they provide a new definition of the situation for the actors.[7] The five levels of task activity for an individual are defined as follows:

(1) *Self-oriented* (not in role) work is personally need-oriented and unrelated to group work.

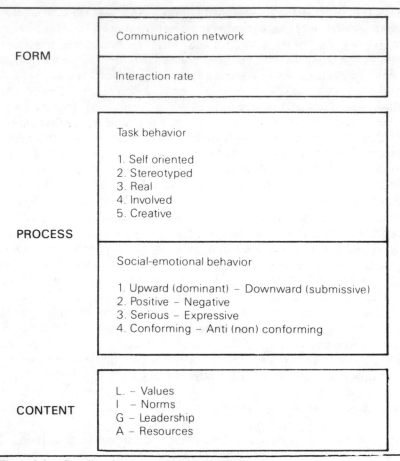

Figure 1.1   Paradigm for the Analysis of Social Interaction

(2)   *Stereotyped* work is maintaining or routine in character.

(3)   *Real* work may involve attempting to define the task, searching for a methodology, or clarifying already established plans.

(4)   *Involved* work is group-focused and introduces some new ingredient: active problem-solving.

(5)   *Creative* work is highly insightful and integrative. It often interprets what has been going on in the group and brings together in a meaningful way a series of experiences.

For the analysis of case material—as in the chapters in Part II—the level of creative involvement of the principal actors and groups can be illustrated by preparing a graph with the level of creativity as the vertical axis, and time as the horizontal axis. The division of the total action into acts and scenes can be noted on the time line, and the rising and falling levels of creativity for each of the actors can be indicated during each of these time periods.

If the group as a unit is the actor or image carrier, then the set of categories is similar except that the rating is made of the extent of the creativity of the small group in relation to the work or activity of a larger organization or collective activity. For example, the first category becomes "*group-oriented*—work is related to the needs of the small group and not to the needs of the larger organization or collectivity." In either case, work at the highest level can provide a new image that redefines the situation as a focus for a new set of roles enacted in the form of a new "play."

The five levels of involvement and creativity for the individual at the group level are similar to the five levels of creativity identified by Taylor (1975: 306-308) to describe the work of scientists, craftpersons, and artists, who make contributions to a whole society:

(1) *Expressive:* spontaneity, where originality and quality of the product are unimportant (as in children's drawings).

(2) *Technical:* involving skill and a new level of proficiency (for example, Stradivari's violin).

(3) *Inventive:* ingenuity with materials, providing combinations to solve old problems in new ways (examples: Edison's light and Bell's telephone).

(4) *Innovative:* basic principles are understood so that modification through alternative approaches is possible (example: Jung and Adler elaborate on Freud).

(5) *Emergentive:* involves the most abstract ideational principles or assumptions underlying a body of art or science. In rare instances there is an emergence of an entirely new principle or assumption (examples: Einstein, Freud, Picasso).

These five levels of creativity for a whole society can be used to indicate the overall impact of a particular conflict or instance of conflict resolution. In some of the cases described in Part II, we shall see that some of the agreements reached to settle a conflict are at a low level of creativity because they do not solve the issue but simply postpone settlement until a later time, other solutions provide combinations or extensions of existing ideas, and some may even introduce entirely new concepts. We would expect a positive correlation between the level of creativity of the solution and the effectiveness of the solution in avoiding a resumption of the conflict over the same

TABLE 1.1   Interaction Process Analysis, Four Dimensions

I.   Upward vs. Downward

Upward:	Assuming autocratic control or seeking status in the group by making direct suggestions or by giving opinions that serve to guide group activity. (Also measured by total talking rate.)
Downward:	Showing dependence by asking for help, showing anxiety, shame and guilt, or frustration, laughing at the jokes of a dominant person.

II.   Positive vs. Negative

Positive:	Seeming friendly by showing affection, agreement, or by asking for information or opinion in an encouraging way.
Negative:	Seeming unfriendly by disagreeing, showing antagonism, or diffuse aggression.

III.   Serious vs. Expressive

Serious:	Giving information or opinions that indicate serious involvement in the task. Routine agreement.
Expressive:	Giving support to others regardless of task performance or showing tension release through joking or other evidence of flight from the task.

IV.   Conforming vs. Anticonforming

Conforming:	Seeking to be guided by the group norms by asking for information or suggestions. Making jokes or dramatic statements that reveal the basic nature of the group.
Anticonforming:	Showing tension that indicates withdrawal from the field. Describing fantasies that reveal individual goals rather than group goals. Resisting pressure to conform.

SOURCE: Reprinted with permission of publisher from: Hare, A.P. Four dimensions of interpersonal behavior. *Psychological Reports,* 1972, 30, 499-512, Figure 10.

issue, with the most effective solutions providing a new "non-zero-sum" definition of the situation in which all of the previously conflicting parties realize some gain.

Within the social-emotional area, the four process dimensions that appear most frequently in the social psychological literature are upward-downward (dominant-submissive), positive-negative, serious-expressive, and conforming-anti(non)conforming (Hare, 1982: 38-40). A brief description of the end points of each of the four dimensions is given in Table 1.1, and an indication of a seven-point scale that could be used to rate an actor on each dimension is given in Table 1.2. Bales and Cohen (1979; Bales, 1984) build their "new field theory" on the first two of these dimensions plus a third dimension, forward-backward, that combines the last two dimensions. That is, "forward" behavior is serious and conforming whereas "backward" behavior is expressive and nonconforming.[8]

For the analysis of the *content* of the interaction, a set of four categories can be used that is based on the four functional problems of groups (see Parsons, 1961): (L) the members must develop some common identity and some commitment to the values of the group, (I)

TABLE 1.2   Four Dimensions: Observer's Recording Sheet

	Subject Rating
I. Upward-Downward	
Very dominant – more dominant than necessary, pushing, not allowing others to speak, shouting.	7
Dominant – continually initiating conversation, blocking path.	6
Slightly dominant – any slight hint of dominance, approaching the other person, occasionally initiating dialogue.	5
Neutral	4
Slightly submissive – the slightest bit submissive, hesistating, avoiding looking at the other person.	3
Submissive – backing off, obviously avoiding the other person, speaking only when spoken to, acknowledging an order.	2
Very submissive – running away, cringing.	1
II. Positive-Negative	
Very positive – "gushing," hugging, kissing, other signs of extreme affection.	7
Positive – agreeing, smiling, encouraging, overt signs of friendliness.	6
Slightly positive – the slightest signs of friendliness, smiling, being pleasant.	5
Neutral	4
Slightly negative – not smiling, gloomy.	3
Negative – hostile, challenging, disagreeing.	2
Very negative – nasty, angry.	1
III. Serious-Expressive	
Very serious – soberly involved in the task with indications of high inertia, i.e., would be difficult to move to a lighter vein. Indications of anxiety about turning from task.	7
Serious – giving information or opinions that indicate serious involvement in the task.	6
Slightly serious – routine agreement or other indications that individual is paying attention to the work.	5
Neutral	4
Slightly expressive – smiling or other indications that individual finds situation amusing and is not very involved.	3
Expressive – joking and laughing or other forms or relief from the tension of the serious nature of the task.	2
Very expressive – giving support to others regardless of task performance. Obvious signs of flight from the task (through fantasy or acting out) that make it difficult for others to do serious work.	1

TABLE 1.2 (Continued)

	Subject Rating
IV. Conforming-Anticonforming	
Very conforming – clear statements or action indicating that others should stay in line with group norms.	7
Conforming – seeking to be guided by group norms by asking for information or suggestions. Revealing a constriction of fantasy life and social patterns in line with group norms.	6
Slightly conforming – acting in an accepted way for this group, especially in response to requests for conformity.	5
Neutral	4
Slightly anticonforming – shows tension or slight resistance to group activity.	3
Anticonforming – acting in ways that are clearly different from majority, although within accepted limits for the group as a whole.	2
Very anticonforming – withdrawing from the field, describing fantasies that reveal individual goals rather than group goals. Urging anarchistic values.	1

they must develop rules that allow them to coordinate their activity and enough feeling of solidarity to stay together to complete the task, (G) they must be able to exercise enough control over their membership to be effective in reaching their common goal, and (A) they must have or be able to generate the skills and resources necessary to reach the group goal (Hare, 1982: 25). The content of the functional categories as they would be used for the analysis of behavior in small groups or small social systems is given in Table 1.3.

The listing of the four categories L, I, G, and A in the preceding paragraph and in Table 1.3 (from top to bottom) is given in the order of the "cybernetic hierarchy of control" where parts of a system that are high in *information* control those that are high on *energy* (Hare, 1982: 24-26; 1983a: 432-433). The classic everyday example is that of the rider with ideas about where to go (information) being able to control the direction of the horse (energy). An example from a physical system is the thermostat that processes information about temperature that is able to control a furnace that produces heat (Effrat, 1976: 666-669).

The hypothesis that the concept of a cybernetic hierarchy applies to the L, I, G, and A categories is used in the analysis of different types of persuasion (Hare, 1982: 90-108; 1983a: 434-442) and to rank order the four major functional substructures of the social system according to their relative influence on social behavior: L—religious, I—legal, G—political, and A—economic (Hare, 1982: 22-24; 1983a: 430-431). The same concept of a hierarchy applies to the four major

TABLE 1.3   Functional Categories for Small Group Analysis

L	+	Seeks or provides basic categories or ultimate values
		    Asks for or seeks to define:
		        basic purpose or identity of group
		        fundamental meaning of "all this"
		        general orientation
		        basic obligations

	−	Seeks to deny, take away, or inhibit the development and recognition of values.

I	+	Seeks or provides solidarity or norms (as primary mechanism of conflict management)
		    Asks for or seeks to define:
		        how the group can get along better, promote harmony, or decrease conflict.
		        what the specific norms governing relations should be

	−	Seeks to deny, inhibit, or prevent the formation of norms and movement toward group solidarity

G	+	Seeks or provides relatively specific direction, goal-definition, or problem solutions relevant to the group's goals.
		    Asks for or seeks to define:
		        relatively specific group goals (be careful to distinguish from values and norms)
		        decisions which in effect are attainment of group's goals

	−	Seeks to prevent or inhibit movement toward the group's goals

A	+	Seeks or provides facilities for goal attainment
		    Asks for or seeks to define:
		        how to get or increase (especially to generalize) resources, relevant information, or facts

	−	Seeks to deny, inhibit, or prevent the provision of facilities and relevant information

SOURCE: A Paul Hare, "Group Decision by Consensus," *Sociological Inquiry* 43 (1973). Reprinted by permission from the publisher, the University of Texas Press.

systems that affect behavior: L—culture, I—social system, G—personality, and A—biological system. The values represented by the culture are more controlling than the norms of the social system. The norms of the social system are in turn more controlling than the personality of the individual. Finally, the personality characteristics play a more controlling part in social interaction than the biological traits and processes of the physical organism.

Although the terms are used in Table 1.3 with meanings that are not exactly the same as in Parsons's original formulations (see Parsons, 1961) as they were applied to large social units, the names of the categories are still the same. L stands for "latent pattern maintenance and tension management," I stands for "integration," G stands for "goal attainment," and A stands for "adaptation."

TABLE 1.4   Sixteen Types of Roles (Images) Classified According to
Four Dimensions of Interpersonal Behavior

Dimensional Code	Examples of Roles (images)
1. UPSC	Natural leader
2. UNSC	Dictator, prison warden
3. UNEC	Exhibitionist
4. UPEC	Inspirational leader, old-fashioned mother, doctor
5. DPSC	Nurse, mail man, over achiever
6. DNSC	Spy, informer
7. DNEC	Critic, help-rejecting-complainer
8. DPEC	Clinging vine, yes-man
9. UPSA	Idealist, agent of change
10. UNSA	Anarchist, revolutionary
11. UNEA	Playboy, motorcycle bum
12. UPEA	Joker, court jester
13. DPSA	Pacifist, nonviolent resister
14. DNSA	Skeptic
15. DNEA	Defector, deserter, rebel
16. DPEA	Kept woman, gigolo

NOTE: U = upward (dominant); D = downward (submissive); P = positive; N = negative; S = serious; E. = expressive; C = conforming; A = anti(non)conforming.

For the analysis of group development the functional categories describe the focus of behavior during five acts (stages, phases) that typically occur in groups. In the first act, the purpose of the group is defined and the commitment of the members secured (L); in the second act, resources or skills must be provided or acquired (A); in the third act, roles related to the task must be developed and a high level of morale achieved (I); and in the fourth act, the group works on the task with the coordination of its leadership (G). These four stages may be repeated as a group takes on new tasks in turn. Within each major stage one can usually identify four substages occurring in the same order. Eventually at the end of the group's life there is a terminal phase, a last act, in which the group redefines the relationships between members as the group is disbanded (terminal L) (Hare, 1982: 68-89; 1983a: 433-439). A more detailed description of the functional categories as they apply to Smelser's (1962) discussion of the cybernetic hierarchy and group development in collective behavior is given in Appendix 2.

Although no typology of roles has yet been developed that combines all the aspects of form, process, and content, role systems of various degrees of complexity have been formulated that focus on the social-emotional dimensions of process and the functional categories of content (Hare, 1982: 122-138). When social psychologists or persons from the theater do offer role typologies, they are more likely to stress the process than the content (see Appendix 1 and Chapter 2). Thus most of the role types mentioned in the literature can be found somewhere on the list of 16 types of roles or images given in Table 1.4. The table was developed by first dichotomizing each of the four dimensions of social interaction and then noting the role types that would appear in each sector of the four-dimensional social space. Directions for plotting the behavior of persons filling these roles on a field diagram and analyzing their interrelationships are given further along in this chapter.

Roles can be played out at one system level or they can have implications for several system levels at the same time. The themes that are enacted may involve the whole planet, some environmental or cultural area, a whole society, a functional segment of a society, an organization, a functional segment of an organization, or a small group. One can even focus on the various roles played by a single individual.

Organizations and Networks

Some of the basic elements in the structure of formal organizations and in informal networks or events involving some form of collective behavior (crowds, demonstrations, riots, etc.) are given in Figure 1.2. From the dramaturgical point of view, the elements are essentially the same whether we are looking at a formal organization, such as a university or a motor car factory, or an instance of collective behavior, such as a protest demonstration. They involve both groups and individuals in the roles of directors, protagonists, auxiliary players, and audiences, and take place in some stage setting. The differences lie in the permanency of the role relationships and the degree of preparation involved for playing each role, both of which are usually greater for the formal organization.

Also indicated in Figure 1.2 are the reference groups that help to sustain role performance even though the members may not be part of the organization under analysis. For example, some of the role expectations for workers in a motor factory are set by fellow members of unions that include workers from other organizations. Some of the expectations for the role of management may come from managers of other enterprises who meet socially at the local country club.

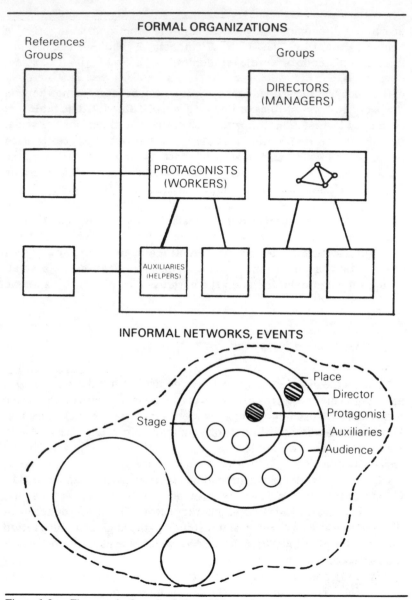

Figure 1.2   Elements in Organizations and Networks

However formal or informal the role relationships, individuals do not learn single roles, but sets of related roles. In instances of collective behavior, an individual may shift instantly from one role to another, for example, from audience member to auxiliary to pro-

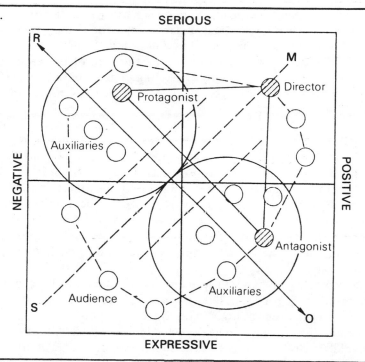

SERIOUS

NEGATIVE — POSITIVE

EXPRESSIVE

R

M

Director

Protagonist

Auxiliaries

Antagonist

Audience

Auxiliaries

S

O

Figure 1.3   Small Groups

tagonist. This is less likely to happen without a period of formal training in an organization, although in a crisis situation, such as during actual battle for a military organization, role shifts may also be instantaneous.

Although most of the literature on roles focuses on the individual in a role in a small group or larger organization, sets of persons (groups) also play roles (have functions) in formal organizations and informal networks. All of the same concepts that are used to describe the role of the individual as an actor in the small group can also be used to describe the small group as an actor in a large organization.

Small Groups

A closer look at the roles within a small group is provided in Figure 1.3. The conventions used to plot the roles in this field diagram are those developed by Bales and Cohen (1979) to illustrate the parts played by members of "self-analytic" groups of students in classes on interpersonal relations at Harvard University. The horizontal axis represents the negative-positive dimension of the interpersonal space (from left to right). The vertical axis represents the serious-expressive dimension (from top to bottom). The dimension of upward-downward (dominant-submissive) is indicated by the size of the circle that surrounds the dot (or small circle) locating a person or role on the first two dimensions. The larger circles represent the more upward (dominant) members.

To simplify the diagram, the ratings for conforming-anticonforming are not shown in Figure 1.3. We might assume that in this example all the group members are conforming and therefore undifferentiated on the fourth dimension. However if ratings on conformity were needed, they could be indicated by a number—representing the degree of conformity—placed near the dot that shows the location of the individual on the plane of the field diagram. Any other set of marks or colors could also be used. For example, the circles for the conformists might be white, the anticonformists black, and persons who are neutral, blue.

Each dimension can be represented by a seven-point scale (as illustrated in Table 1.2). The two axes of serious-expressive and positive-negative can be divided into seven units with the number 4 at the center. The circles can be depicted in seven different sizes, with the smallest circle representing the submissive end of the continuum. The rating on conformity can be indicated by a number from 1 to 7.[9]

Whatever method is used to indicate the degree of conformity on the field diagram, the result will be to highlight the presence of two subgroups within the larger group. One set, given as Types 1-8 in Table 1.4, are the conformists who stand ready to maintain the status quo. The other set, given as Types 9-16 in the table, are the anticonformists who do not support the status quo and are more open to social change, in some cases actively proposing it. Thus, if one were trying to compose a group to work on a well-defined task on which all members might be expected to agree, one would choose persons who could play roles of Types 1-8. On the other hand, if one wanted to open a new frontier or to organize a movement for social change, then one might recruit persons who could play roles of Types 9-16. For maximum creativity, all types are needed—the anticonformists to come up with new ideas and the conformists to shape them and enact them (Hare, 1982: 136).

Also shown in Figure 1.3 are some lines and circles that represent the extent and direction of *polarization* and *unification* in the group. Bales believes that, especially for the type of classroom group that he observes, there is a continual swing back and forth between polarization and unification when all group members are supporting the same image. When there are two opposing images in a group, the direction of opposition can be indicated by the *Line of Polarization* (the solid line tipped with arrowheads at both ends) that passes across the field diagram in a direction that is located by a procedure described in Bales's book. One end of the Line of Polarization is marked with an "R," which stands for *reference direction*. The other end of the line of polarization is marked with an "O," which stands for *opposite direction*. In the fictitious example of a "self-analytic" seminar at a university that is given in Figure 1.3 the reference direction is serious and negative (representing a main image of work under authoritarian leadership). The opposite direction is expressive and positive (representing an anti-authoritarian, more playful image). The most dominant person in each subgroup is likely to be the protagonist (image carrier) for that subgroup. In this case, the theme carrier in the opposite direction is the "antagonist" of the image carrier in the reference direction, but he or she might, in another situation, represent a different image, rather than one that was mainly antagonistic to the main image.

A dashed line, called the *line of balance*, passes across the field diagram at right angles to the line of polarization. One end of the line of balance is marked with an "M," which stands for *mediator direction*, and the other end with an "S," which stands for *scapegoat direction*. These terms have reference to the possible social psychological significance of any person, role, or image that is "far out" in one direction or the other. An example will be given when considering Bales's heuristic hypotheses below.

There are two large circles on the diagram, one on each side of the line of balance, each centered on the line of polarization. These represent the two polar fields of polarization. The circle nearest the "R" is called the *reference circle*, and the one nearest the "O," the *opposite circle*. In the kit that Bales supplies for the analysis of groups using his method, these lines and circles are marked on a plastic sheet that can be used as an overlay for another sheet of paper, in standard format, on which the positions of the group members or roles have been indicated in terms of the three interpersonal dimensions. The plastic overlay sheet is rotated over the paper with the diagram of positions in the group to a position such that most of the group members appear in one or the other of the large circles. The degree of polarization is then judged by the "goodness of fit." If most of the persons in the group appear within the two circles, as in this example, then the group is considered to be polarized; however, if the persons do not fall clearly into two or more subgroups, then the group may be unified.

In Figure 1.3 there are also two short dashed lines on either side of the line of balance and parallel to it. Between them is the *swing area*. In a case of conflict between subgroups persons in this area may be rejected by both sides, or they may decide to "swing" their votes to one side or the other.

Two other kinds of relationships are also indicated in the diagram. The center points of the circles representing the three most dominant persons are connected with solid lines to show the *dominant triangle*, as these persons have most to do with the direction of group activity. In the example given here, the three most dominant persons are the protagonist in the reference circle, the antagonist in the opposite circle, and the teacher (director) who happens to be located in the mediator direction.

A dotted line connects those persons who are most distant from the center of the total constellation of image points. This is called the *perimeter*. The perimeter may call attention to some moderate or low participants who are nevertheless salient because they are "far out" in their given direction. These persons may represent the limits of role behavior that is acceptable for membership in this group.

Six Heuristic Hypotheses

Bales does not use terms such as protagonist, auxiliary, and audience in his analysis of interpersonal behavior; however his hypotheses concerning behavior in groups can easily be used as a source of insight for dramaturgical analysis with minimal changes in terminology. For example, Bales offers six heuristic hypotheses as a way to begin to predict some of the developments in a group once a diagram, such as that in Figure 1.3, has been drawn that could be based on observations in early sessions of the group, or perhaps on personality assessments or self-ratings made before the first session of the group. The heuristic hypotheses are as follows (Bales and Cohen, 1979: 58-108):

(1) Dominant members may clash early, especially if they are in different quadrants of the space. (That is, dominant members in different quadrants are likely to be protagonists for different images of behavior).

(2) Far-out members may clash sooner or later, that is, in the middle period of a chronically polarized group. (The far-out members could be persons who initially take an audience or auxiliary role, but whose

needs are not actually met by the main image carriers. Sooner or later they may wish to assert themselves).

(3) Downward members may come in last, although the leader could help bring them in. (These are probably persons who are content to remain in an audience role and whose skills may therefore be under-utilized by the group).

(4) Salient images may polarize or unify the group. (This is a central proposition in dramaturgical analysis. Salient images provide the focus for a set of roles that make it possible to enact a play. More than one play may take place at the same time).

(5) Polarization may tend to create leaders and subgroups. (As a drama-turgical hypothesis, this would be stated the other way around. Leaders (image carriers) and subgroups that form around them (auxiliaries and audiences) tend to create polarization).

(6) Polarization may be neutralized by mediation, scape-goating, or domination. (In each case a super-ordinate goal—image—is presented that calls for a new role set that includes all the members of the group and provides unity).

In contrast to Bales and others who observe behavior in a group and make a judgement about the role an individual was playing when the behavior is summarized at the end of a session, the dramaturgical approach requires the observer to consider the roles being played by group members at the moment of their action. The set of roles being considered may be simple or complex, but it is assumed that collective behavior can only take place when individuals relate to each other in roles. In the example in Figure 1.3, the parts being played are indicated by a minimum set of roles: director, protagonist, antagonist, auxiliary, and audience. If this diagram included all the persons present in a classroom, and there was a clear "action area" such that some persons were "onstage," whereas others were "offstage" in the audience, or "backstage" warming up for their parts, then these areas could also be indicated in the field diagram (see Goffman, 1959, for examples of these kinds of activities). Although Bales has done most of his analysis at the small group level, his groups actually provide a microcosm of larger social systems and of spontaneous forms of collective behavior.

Summary

As an introduction to a dramaturgical perspective on social inter-action, three sets of concepts are presented: first, a suggestion on the range of ideas around which social interaction is organized. An image provides a focus of attention in a small informal group; a theme is the focus in collective behavior such as an acting crowd; a plot in a social movement; and a script gives the most detailed description of role behavior in an organization.

Second, is a basic list of roles and aspects of the situation that influence the development of the ideas. As a new idea is first presented, there is a protagonist who introduces the idea and an audience who hears about it. Members of the audience may take roles in support of or against the idea as auxiliaries. A person who takes the lead in opposing a new idea becomes the antagonist. There may be a director who helps organize the activity. There may also be a playwright who is the author of the new idea but does not enact it. The action takes place on a stage that sets broad limits on the kinds of activity that can be developed. Persons may behave differently onstage, offstage, and backstage. The time available for a presentation is always limited, ranging from a few seconds to a life time.

Third, an indication of the elements of the form, process, and content of social interaction exists that should be considered when describing its dramatic development. Form has two aspects, the communication network and interaction rate. Process also has two aspects, task behavior coded by its degree of creativity and social-emotional behavior coded along four dimensions: dominant-submissive, positive-negative, serious-expressive, and conforming-anticonforming. Content is coded according to the four functional problems of groups: latent pattern maintenance, integration, goal attainment, and adaptation.

Although no scheme for describing role types has yet been developed that incorporates all of the elements of social interaction, ratings on the four dimensions of social-emotional behavior can be used to describe many of the images and roles that appear in everyday life and in the theater. In formal organizations the roles are usually clearly identified and learned. In formal networks or events, roles may be assumed momentarily, but a similar cast of directors, protagonists, auxiliaries, and audience members appears in both. For analysis, it is helpful to plot the images and roles on a field diagram that indicates the degree of unification or polarization in a group and to consider the applicability of the six heuristic hypotheses suggested by Bales.

Notes

1. Boulding (1956: Ch. 1) discusses the images (knowledge about) that people have of their physical environment, roles, interpersonal relations, and place in time. He lists some of the relationships that may exist between new images produced in a group and existing images. The new information may do the following:

    (a) leave the present images unaffected

(b) change the image in some way

(c) produce a radical reformulation

(d) clarify in that it makes some aspect of the existing image more certain

2. Berger and Luckman (1967: 75) in their analysis of the social construction of reality underline the importance of the script in their observation that:

> Only through . . . representation in performed roles can the institution manifest itself in actual experience. The institution with its assemblage of "programmed" actions, is like the unwritten libretto of a drama. The realization of the drama depends upon the reiterated performance of its prescribed roles by living actors. The actors embody the roles and actualize the drama by representing it on a given stage. Neither the drama nor institution exist empirically apart from this recurrent realization.

However even in organizations, as well as in small groups, instances of collective, and social movements, it is well to be reminded that there may be more than one script, plot, theme, or image, as indicated in the analyses of cases in the chapters on conflict and conflict resolution. For some analysts, the conflict is a more fundamental phenomenon than the stability in a system. Lyman and Scott (1970: 5) using the metaphor of a "game" for their analysis of social interaction conclude that:

> If life consists of encounters, episodes and engagements among persons pursuing goals of which they are consciously aware, or about which they can be made aware, then it appears that the fundamental structure of human action is conflict.

3. Research on cognition and artificial intelligence emphasizes the importance of the definition of the situation as an "orienting schema" that is an "active, information-seeking structure" (Neisser, 1976: 111). "Variants of the context-sensitive processing are often referred to as *top-down, hierarchal, model-driven, or knowledge-driven* control structures" (McArthur, 1982: 295). Winston (1977: 180) gives an indication of how the process works:

> When one encounters a new situation (or makes a substantial change in one's view of a problem), one selects from memory a structure called a *frame*. This is a remembered framework to be adapted to fit reality by changing the details as necessary. A *frame* is a data-structure for representing a stereotyped situation like being in a certain kind of living room or going to a child's birthday party. . . . The "top levels" of a frame are fixed, and represent things that are always true about the supposed situation. The lower levels have many *terminals*—"slots" that must be filled by specific instances or data.

4. This is true for all societies. In a discussion of the nature of social interaction, Parsons (1968: 438ff.) notes:

> The phenomenon of *role pluralism* is a central feature of all human societies, and this is more important the more highly developed the society. . . . Thus, the unit of collectivity membership is not *the individual* in general but the *person in role*.

5. The connection between ideas and enactments does appear in the anthropological literature, especially in the analysis of the ritual behavior (Turner, 1974). Lyman and Scott (1975: 115-127) provide an example in the political area in their discussion of the dramatization of political myths that are used to legitimate different types of authority. They describe six myths that provide moral justification for the ruler: (1) wisdom and knowledge, (2) divine sanction, (3) courage and heroism, (4) consent and majority rule, (5) tradition and custom, and (6) inevitable historical forces.

Edelman (1977) and Rothman (1981) have also noted some of the ways that political settings and behavior are organized to symbolize political ideas.

Political settings in the United States "are unabashedly built up to emphasize a departure from men's daily routine, a special or heroic quality in the proceedings they are to frame. Massiveness, ornateness, and formality are the most common notes struck in the design of these scenes, and they are presented on a scale which focuses constant attention upon the difference between everyday life and the special occasion when one appears in court, in Congress, or at an event of historic significance (Edelman, 1977: 96).

6. If the group under observation is not autonomous but is responsible to an individual or organization that provides funds and sets overall guidelines for action, then the role of *producer* can be added to this basic list. In the theater the producer provides the backing for the play. The influence of the producer may not be visible to the audience but financial limitations may well have determined the size of the cast and the elaborateness of the setting.

7. These categories were adapted from those developed by Thelen et al. in 1951 (Stock and Thelen, 1958: 193; see Hare, 1982: 45, for an indication of the relationship). However up to 1969 at least so little attention had been given to the subject of creativity in everyday activities that Argyle (1973: 13-14) was moved to remark: "there is presumably creativity in social behavior, as in other kinds of behavior, but nothing is known about it yet."

8. My reasons for using four rather than three dimensions have been given in a previous publication (Hare, 1982: 36-37). Bales and Cohen (1979: 264-265) report that in some of their studies the third factor that they use in their ratings splits into two again, giving them four factors, with the fourth factor accounting for 2.6–6.4 percent of the variance. They acknowledge that the backward direction of their third factor has two logically disparate components and that the fourth factor they find may be related to one of these. It appears to be the emotional aspect of counteraction to control. In other words, the two components of "expressive" and "anticonforming" that were combined reappear.

Some of the research that also reports variations of the four dimensions has already been reviewed (Hare, 1976: 69-80; 1982: 38-40). Similar findings are reported by Wish and Kaplan (1977).

9. When numbers from 1 to 7 are used, the number 7 is used to represent the "high" or "positive" end of the dimension and the number 1 to represent the "low" or "negative" end of the dimension. Thus if act by act ratings are made of interaction (see example in Hare, 1982: 49) or are used as summary ratings of behavior in some of the examples in this volume, a high number is associated with a high degree of dominance, positiveness, seriousness, or conformity. If these rating scales are used in some research where the results will be correlated with other variables, then using the numbers in this way will give the ordinary meaning to positive and negative correlations because high scores on other variables will be associated with high scores on these four rating scales.

Chapter 2

Perspectives from the Theater

In this chapter, we turn to the theater for additional concepts and insights that will be useful for the analysis of social interaction. After first considering some comments about the theatrical event, the types of theater, and the relationship between theatrical performances and everyday life, we will note in turn the function of the stage, the roles of playwright, director, actor, and audience member, and the development of the play throughout a series of scenes and acts.

The Theatrical Event

Although others (see Schechner, 1973; Innes, 1981) have noted the similarity between performances of actors in the theater and those of persons who make imagined visits to the spirit world, Cole (1975) presents more detail than most concerning the nature of the similarity. This type of visitation can in turn be seen as a representation of the steps in any type of creativity. It involves some form of warm up, insight, and the transmission of the new idea to an audience (Hare, 1982: 158-159). But before taking the second step, let us take the first by following Cole's analysis of the theatrical event.

For Cole (1975: 8) the theater provides an opportunity of experiencing imaginative truth as present truth. At many points in history and in many parts of the world, people have believed that there is an "illud tempus," a time of origins, a period of creation. Creation continues because it is the place "where it is always happening." This illud tempus is a place in space but it is also a place within the individual that is accessible through dreams and illusions. In some societies there is a person, the shaman, who specializes in going into a trance state when his soul is believed to leave his body and ascend to the sky or descend to the underworld to visit the illud tempus. Because the illud tempus is also within the person, the visit is also an inner journey. Because the shaman's double voyage is on behalf of the audience, he makes it possible that "we go there."

A variation on this voyage is enacted by the hungan, a person who specializes in becoming "possessed." Although "hungan" is the Haitian term for the priest of a possession cult, Cole uses it to refer to all persons who play a similar role. The hungan is a human being whose presence becomes, through possession, a god's presence. He makes it possible that "they come here."

Cole suggests that the two roles, of shaman and hungan, are in effect assumed by the same person at different points in the voyage. A person in search of insight is like the shaman going to a distant place. On reaching the place where creativity is always occurring, the person has a creative shift in perception, and then turns back, or "rounds." The return trip is in the role of hungan, one who is possessed of the new insight.

Cole (1975: 54) describes "rounding" as "the moment when the quest can go no further, the spirit held no longer, the magic accomplish no more. To round at that moment . . . to become a hungan, a mere vehicle, is the price the shaman must pay for having attained his goal."

Like the shaman, the actor on the stage must draw on his own inner experience to present the image that his role requires. "For the actor as for the shaman," Cole (1975: 22) observes,

> an inward journey is the sole means by which a journey can be performed on behalf of others. The shaman can explore the archetypal world of the illud tempus only be seeking those archetypes in his own fantasies, memories, and dreams. The actor can explore an illud tempus which is the work of another man's imagination only be exploring his own psyche for answering impulses, shared fantasies, common symbolisms.

For the individual in the small group, the images represent ideas brought forward from past experience or insights of the moment that are "made present" in the group. Thus both shaman and actor make explicit the process of presenting an "image" that Bales has observed in the small group.

In real life, people tend to keep their distance from shamans and hungans. Cole (1975: 64) believes that the fact that many people are a little leery of mingling with actors after a stage performance results from the similarity in function. The ambivalent response of an audience to an actor combines gratitude that he has made the image present with mistrust of what he has become in the course of doing so.

Although Cole was referring to the theater, his central focus on the "image," and the roles that people play in support of an image, illustrates the central idea in the dramaturgical perspective as we are using it. In contrast to Polti (1977), who described thirty-six dramatic situations, Cole (1975: 161) asserted that "there are not thirty-six dramatic situations, but one: an image would be presented."

Types of Plays

Hamilton (1939: 17) defines a play as "a representation, by actors, on a stage, before an audience, of a struggle between individual human wills, motivated by emotion rather than intellect, and expressed in terms of objective action." He notes that in the four types of plays that are usually identified in histories of drama through the nineteenth century, in two—namely tragedy and comedy—the characters control the plot, and in the other two—melodrama and farce—the plot controls the characters (Hamilton, 1939: 72-75). Tragedy and melodrama tend to be serious with an unhappy ending in contrast to comedy and farce that have a lightness of style and a happy ending (Sobel, 1959).

Bentley (1967: 197-308) also discusses these four types of drama at some length, observing that comedy provides hope because it takes place on the other side of disaster; the transcending emotion is joy. Fry (1962: 68) elaborates on this theme. Both tragedy and comedy deal with truth, but "comedy is an escape, not from truth but from despair: a narrow escape into faith . . . In tragedy we suffer pain; in comedy pain is a fool, suffered gladly.

In the twentieth century, the distinctions between these four forms and other newer forms became increasingly blurred (Sobel, 1959:

128). However the early dramatists seem to have anticipated a current set of ideas in social psychology that are brought together under the label of "attribution theory" (Raven and Rubin, 1983: 103-118). In attribution theory, all outcomes are divided by ordinary people into two types, bad and good. People then attempt to find a cause to which they can attribute the outcome. The causes also tend to be classified as one of two types, either some person, the self or another, or the situation. These two dichotomies provide a fourfold classification that is essentially the same as that for the four types of drama: Tragedy has a bad outcome attributed to some person or persons, comedy a good outcome also attributed to the character or personality of a person, melodrama has a bad outcome attributed to the situation in which the actors find themselves, and farce has a good outcome also dominated by the situation.

In everyday life it is perhaps easiest to identify events of a tragic nature, especially when one or more persons are killed because of some "fatal flaw" in the character of a person. The interethnic conflicts and conflicts between protestors and police that are described in Part II of this volume have a more melodramatic nature because persons are playing out social roles with little attention to personality differences. Persons who suddenly find themselves in embarrassing situations or are the butt of practical jokes become the actors in farcical events. Finally, those occasions when people can gain enough distance on their problems to be able to laugh at them in song, cartoons, mime, or free-flowing dialogue provide the essence of comedy.

Each of the various social psychological theories seem to take one of these four types of drama as a set of basic assumptions concerning the nature of human nature and the relation of the individual to the group. For the Freudians, life is essentially tragic, the playing out of drives within the individual. For the Marxians, life is melodramatic. The major forces at work are represented by class conflicts. For the Parsonians, life is more of a farce. Although outcomes can be pleasant, culture and social system variables have more to do with behavior than personality or biological nature. For those subscribing to humanist, symbolic interactionist, or dramaturgical views, the important aspect of life is to be found in its comic nature, when persons can stand apart from interaction, even as they engage in it, to discover its meaning. They enjoy life because, along with Fry, they do not escape from truth, but from despair.

36 Dramatic Situations

In addition to describing the four major types of drama (tragedy, comedy, melodrama, and farce), many writers have suggested that there may be only a limited number of plots. For example, Bentley, quoted above, listed three types of tragedy: (1) suffering and endurance, (2) destruction and renewal, and (3) sacrifice and expiation. Heathcote, who used drama as a learning medium with children, explained to her young actors that there were three kinds of drama: (1) drama that happens because things happen to people that they cannot possibly control (such as a tidal wave or war), (2) where some people start pushing other people around, and (3) where ordinary people find it tricky just to get on together (Wagner, 1979: 21).

One of the most extensive analyses of types of dramatic situations was conducted by Polti in the early 1900s. His work, originally in French, was translated into English in 1921 and republished in 1977. A previous critic of drama had asserted that there were only 36 basic dramatic situations. Polti sought to challenge this statement by categorizing some 1,000 stage plays and 200 other dramatic stories. At the conclusion of his work, Polti decided that there were only 36 dramatic situations after all. However he suggested that variations on the 36 situations could be created by altering: (1) ties of friendship or kinship, (2) the degree of consciousness or free will, (3) the energy of the acts that must result, and (4) the parts, so that a group of characters is substituted for an individual (1977: 119). He further noted that most plays are combinations of several dramatic situations; "there is no situation that may not be combined with any other, so that they develop logically, or pose a dilemma, or each pertains to a particular group or a particular role" (1977: 120).

The common theme in all of the situations, Polti concluded, was that every dramatic situation springs from a conflict between two principle directions of effort. At the curtain rise, one of these pre-exists, at the arrival of the other (innocent or responsible person) the struggle begins. One is the protagonist and the other is the antagonist. Disequilibrium arises from the introduction of a material object, circumstance, or third person, giving a "plot." Some of the additional roles support the protagonist and some the antagonist. These additional auxiliary roles include parts for choruses, confidants, crowds, clowns, and "figurants" (prophets or porters who are precursors of important persons). The same person may play many roles and the same role played by many persons (1977: 120-123).

Polti's work was published long before Parsons emphasized the importance of the four system levels (biological, personality, social system, and culture; see Effrat, 1968) for the analysis of social behavior, and long before Bales and Cohen (1979) introduced the field diagram as a method for the analysis of roles in groups. It is now possible to consider Polti's material in the light of these newer perspectives to see if there might indeed be fewer than 36 basic dramatic situations.

The details of my analysis of Polti's material are given in Appendix 3. The result of the analysis was to reveal seven sets of dramatic situations, four at the social system level where the focus was on the interplay of several roles and three at the individual or personality level where the conflict was between different parts of the self. Briefly, the seven sets were as follows:

A. Social system level
    (1) A hero (upward, positive, serious) as protagonist, a villain (upward, negative, serious) as antagonist, and a third party or object. Conformity or anticonformity is not a major issue.
    (2) The emphasis is on the relative power of the protagonist (downward) and the antagonist (upward).
    (3) The emphasis is on the positive-negative dimension of social interaction. Persons who should like each other do not. The situations of this type generally involve an imbalance of liking in a triangular relationship.
    (4) The emphasis is on the conforming-anticonforming dimension of social interaction. Although the crime may be of any type, a family member or loved one is usually involved in either adultery or incest.
B. Individual or personality level
    (1) The fatal flaw: The upward, positive, serious ideal self is contrasted with the upward, negative behavior of the protagonist. This is similar to set one at the social system level except that the struggle is between two aspects of the same person.
    (2) Search: The theme emphasizes the upward-downward dimension as the relatively powerless protagonist searches for someone overcoming obstacles.
    (3) Self sacrifice: The theme is of conformity to the ideal self versus some pragmatic action.

As Polti himself noted, any of these seven sets of dramatic situations could be either serious or expressive and thus appear in either a tragedy or melodrama or in a comedy or farce. However from the previous definitions of these four types of plays, we would expect that dramatic situations that focus on the social system level would appear more often in plot-driven dramas, and dramatic situations that focus on the individual or personality level would appear more often in character-driven dramas. In addition both Polti and Bentley indicate that situations built upon love, especially incest and adultery, are more likely to appear in comedy and farce.

The short list of seven sets of dramatic situations suggests that only a small number of principal roles may be necessary to enact the ideas that are presented in any dramatic situation. Just as the four types of plays (tragedy, comedy, melodrama, and farce) provide a typology that can be used to classify situations of everyday social interaction, so can the seven sets of roles within the dramatic situations be used as a typology for identifying the roles that are being played in each of these situations. The role sets can also be used for comparison with the roles included in other typologies of dramatic situations, such as those given by Berne (1964) in his analysis of games people play (see Appendix 1).

Relationship Between Theater and Everyday Life

A few quotations from social scientists on the subject of the relationship between theater and everyday life are included in Appendix 1 of this volume. In the past, the debate among social scientists has centered on the extent to which drama was a metaphor for the way social interaction took place or was actually the way it happened. As we will see in the quotations that follow, theater people have also been concerned with this issue.

- Bentley (1967: 186): "Life is a successful piece of theater in which people sit and stand as they will, in which dialogue is reciprocal, in which people gesticulate at each other, and look each other in the eye, whether from interest, affection or dislike."
- Benedetti (1976): "Acting in real life takes the form of celebration of potency (for example, puberty rites), sympathetic magic (for example, rainmaking), transformation (for example, a masked dance to imper-

sonate gods), impersonation (for example, making fun of important persons), and oral tradition (for example, rhapsodies and minstrels)."

● Hodgson and Richards (1974: 15): "The dramatic experience is an intensification of living experience, realized by the selection and reordering of significant moments, and it exists in the communication between actors and audience physically present in one place. This communication takes place at every level: mental, emotional, physical, visual, aural, and aesthetic."

● Brook (1968: 99): "Anyone interested in processes in the natural world would be greatly rewarded by a study of theatre conditions. His discoveries would be far more applicable to general society than the study of bees or ants. Under the magnifying glass he would see a group of people living all the time according to precise, shared, but unnamed standards."

● Johnstone (1979: 33): In directing improvisation in the theater, Johnstone observed that although the actors were improvising everyday conversations, their action did not seem real. His solution was to tell his actors to assume that each had a slightly different status, or social position, in relation to the others. After this the conversation became authentic. "Suddenly we understood that every inflection and movement implies a status, and that no action is due to chance, or really 'motiveless.'"

From these quotations, we can conclude that real life and theater contain all the same elements (Bentley), but that some of life's occasions are more dramatic than others and involve more conscious acting of roles (Benedetti). If we wish, we could study the everyday activities of a group of actors as a microcosm of the real world (Brook). Because the dramatic experience is an intensification of the living experience (Hodgson and Richards), and actors need to be quite conscious of the techniques that they are using to recreate lifelike experiences (Johnstone), we can also look at theater as a simulation or working model of the basic elements in social interaction. Theater people have found it useful to develop a special language to describe their work. These same terms, such as director, playwright, or protagonist, can be used metaphorically as a set of hypotheses to guide the investigation of social events. As Sarbin has noted (Allen and Scheibe, 1982), metaphors are used in science and other arts to describe new phenomena for which there is no adequate vocabulary. When new concepts are developed to describe the phenomena that we wish to include in our expanded version of social-psychological theory we can use them. In the meantime the theater provides a good working set of concepts that will see us through from the overture until the last curtain call, including what is happening backstage, onstage, and outside the theater.

Merging Theater with Life

Whatever differences may have existed in the past between theater and real life, they may not be with us for very long if some of the more recent trends in theater monopolize the stage. Under various names for their art, groups of actors have been experimenting with ideas that merge theater with life. One trend is called "environmental theater" (Schechner, 1973). In this form of theater, moves are made to bring the audience onto the stage and the stage into the street. Theaters are designed so that the total space is shared by audience and actors. It is no longer "theater in the round" but theater in the midst. On occasion, the performance is stopped until some of the audience members come forward to play auxiliary parts in the action space. The director is especially pleased if at the final curtain the pile of bodies on stage includes both actors and former audience members. If one is unable to distinguish one group from the other by the extent to which they are clothed or unclothed, so much the better. For an especially empathetic audience, the doors of the theater are thrown open and the whole ensemble moves to the street to continue the performance as a happening with a new audience, and possibly new participants, from the townspeople. Once the action moves to the street it becomes "guerrilla theater" or street theater.

One goal of these experimental groups is to return to the parts played by the shamans and hungans of other times and other cultures where the actors took parts in rituals that were important in changing people's attitudes. Because this type of ritual is generally performed in a religious context, Innes (1981) calls this movement within theater the "holy theater." Another goal is to do away with scripts altogether so that the entire performance is improvised. In this "living theater" each actor appears in his or her own persona (Benedetti, 1976: 69).

Stage

In the theater, Brockett (1964: 418) identifies two basic purposes of scene design: "to aid audience understanding and to express the play's qualities. As an aid to understanding, the stage setting may define the time and place of the action, it should clarify the relationship of the offstage and onstage space, and it should assist in establishing characterization." In addition, "a good setting is a visual statement of the values of the script" (1964: 420). Thus the stage and its setting, as Burke (1968: 446) summarized in his concept of the "scene/act ratio," provides a frame for the action.

For dramaturgical analysis of social interaction, the images suggested by the different parts of the stage and the setting can be placed on a four-dimensional field diagram so that their potential influence on the development of the action can be noted.

Playwright

Traditionally there has been one person, the playwright, who not only made the play (including the scenario, acts, sets, and blocking) but also wrote the dialogue (Hamilton, 1939: 8). However in some contemporary theater, this function is taken over by a group of actors who improvise the play. They may follow methods such as those offered by Spolin (1977) in a book on "Improvisation for the theatre," that is based on the same assumption as that of Moreno's (1953) psychodramatic and sociometric techniques: creativity in the form of intuition must be preceded by spontaneity. Spolin (1977: 4) observes that "the intuitive can only respond in immediacy—right now: it comes bearing its gifts in the moment of spontaneity, the moment when we are freed to relate and act, involving ourselves in the moving changing world around us."

Whether created by an individual or a group, the meaning of the play is found in its "commanding image," which is "the *playwright's* insight and intuition, the *play's* essence, and . . . the *interpreter's* sense of the whole" (Clay and Krempel, 1967: 27).[1]

In everyday social interaction, the individual or group that served as playwright may or may not be present at the time of the action. In many small group settings, as in a psychodrama, the playwright is the protagonist who offers the images that provide the focus for the action. In some cases, as in a mass demonstration or riot, the playwright may be visible in the audience, if one knows where to look. Or the playwright, in the form of a provocateur, may be well hidden. In cases of terrorism, the person who inspired and planned the action may take pains not to be anywhere near the scene at the time of its implementation. In any event, it is helpful for the analysis of a case, and for any form of intervention, to know whether or not the principal actors are carrying their own themes or are attempting to be the heroes, villains, or fools in someone else's drama.

Director

The major part of the director's role in the theater is to prepare a play for the stage. The work begins on first reading the play. Miles-Brown (1980: 22) has indicated some of the initial tasks the director must perform:

(1) Find the theme
(2) Observe the plot, subplot, and subtext
(3) Locate the dramatic climaxes
(4) Understand the style, the characters, and the relationships
(5) Visualize the staging

If the play was written some years before, or for an audience with a different cultural background, then the director may have an additional problem of translation. The director may need to learn about the playwright's stage, players, and world, to make sure that a modern audience would see the play as the audience did at the time the play was written (Clay and Krempel, 1967: 43-49).

The director continues to function during the actual performances of the play with "side coaching" to the actors when they are in the wings, before going on or leaving the stage, and critiques at the end of the performance after the audience has left (Spolin, 1977: 18ff.).

In everyday interaction, the person playing the director's role may be in the obvious form of the military commander, the work supervisor, the athletic coach, or the master of ceremonies. However, on other occasions, especially in large protest demonstrations, the key government officials who are directing the government's response, and the persons who are directing the protest may not be visible to the audience or to each other. Electronic communication equipment makes it possible for many people to be in contact with the director without being noticed. Since the early 1970s, when the protest demonstrations at the Republican and Democratic political conventions in Miami, Florida, were "rigged" by the U.S. Government— using a bogus protest group and clever methods of crowd control, with police agents in all the protest groups—it is doubtful that there is a major protest demonstration anywhere in the world today that is as spontaneous as it appears to be.

On the other hand, in small casual groups, a full-time director may not be required, and the role assumed only momentarily by one or more members of the group as it is needed. If the activity is complex, as in the theater, the role of director may be shared by a number of people who have different functions.

Without waiting to be told by social-psychologists, persons involved in political conflicts long ago discovered that it was important to identify, and often do away with, the persons who were acting as directors for the opposing side. Like many volatile chemical elements, the "half-life" of a major political figure is relatively short. Lesser figures who may not appear on the "hit list" may be picked off at public events by police "snatch squads" (Clutterbuck, 1973: 33-44), or by self- or other-appointed persons who claim to be acting in accord with some political ideal.

An analysis of the director's role is essential for understanding the types of cases described in this volume. Although the director may be partially hidden in cases of conflict, in the examples of conflict resolution there are usually one or more persons playing visible "third-party" mediators' roles (see Chapters 4, 5, and 6).

Actors' Roles

Although many types of roles derived from the theater could be described—as we have seen in connection with the analysis of Polti's (1977) 36 types of dramatic situations—the two basic role types that need to be described in any dramaturgical analysis are the roles that are central for the plot and the roles of supporting players. As noted in Chapter 1, the central roles may include one or more protagonists who present the major images that guide the action and antagonists whose major function is to oppose them. In serious situations (tragedy and melodrama), these are the heroes and villains; in expressive situations (comedy and farce), these are the fools. The supporting players, or auxiliaries, may have individual roles in support of a protagonist or an antagonist, or some of them may act together as a chorus. The chorus played an important part in early Greek dramas that were held in large amphitheaters without amplification for the sound. Here, masses of people and voices were used to underscore important aspects of the drama. Choruses still exist formally in musicals and dance. In natural small groups, several individuals may in effect act as a chorus as they "oh" or "ah" at the same time, and in larger gatherings as they chant, sing, or dance in unison. For theatrical performances Van Laan (1970: 17-18) lists three functions that a chorus may have:

(1)   Concentrates the spectators' emotions on particular themes
(2)   Concentrates the spectators' attention on particular events
(3)   Provides an emotional sounding board by expressing in its verbal and physical responses the protagonist's hopes and fears

With regard to level of creativity possible, the role of playwright can introduce the highest level by providing a new understanding of a process or an event (Level 5, as described in Chapter 1). The director can, at most, provide a further interpretation of the definition of the situation provided by the playwright (Level 4). For the actor, some creativity is still required in playing a role, but it is unlikely to go beyond the skill level (Level 3) as the actor brings to bear techniques and personal experience in the interpretation of the role. Stanislavski's book on *Creating a Role* (1961) introduced a whole school of "method" acting that provided training for actors so that they might best use their own feelings and experiences in the enactment of their stage roles. This form of creativity is carried further in forms of drama in which the actors improvise the action. The qualities needed for an actor in this situation are set out by Hodgson and Richards (1974: 11) as follows:

Acting is an interpretation, an impression of aspects of the human situation. It may involve playing the role of another person or it may require the imagined response of one's own person to a mood or set of circumstances. In either case, the qualities needed for the best acting are also those qualities required for the fullest living.

Some of the techniques that Moreno, as a director of psychodrama, used with his protagonists, auxiliaries, and audiences were most probably derived from his earlier experiences as a director of a "spontaneity theater" in Vienna when he was still a medical student (Moreno, 1947). He gave his own description of these techniques in a number of publications (see Moreno, 1969: 239-241). Because these techniques first existed in life, were adapted to the theater, and then to psychodrama, it requires minimal adaptation of the ideas in order to use them again for the analysis of everyday interaction. All of the techniques are used to bring to light the thoughts, feelings, and emotions that might otherwise remain hidden in the interaction process. When these techniques are observed in a real life situation, it helps the observer identify these otherwise hidden dimensions. The main techniques that I have found useful for analysis are the following (Hare, 1982: 44-45):

(1) *Role reversal*—An individual, usually the protagonist, exchanges roles and physical positions with another person. For Moreno (as well as for Mead, Cooley, and the other social interactionists), this form of role taking is the main way in which one person comes to understand the thoughts and feelings of another. In a psychodrama, the protagonist, whose life experience is being reenacted, is often asked to reverse roles with an auxiliary player who has been asked to play some person known only to the protagonist to give the auxiliary an idea of the role he or she is to portray. Real life examples occur often in the family when a child plays a parent and the parent becomes the child.

(2) *Soliloquy*—Verbalizing thoughts and feelings, often while turning the head to one side. In the theater, the protagonist often uses the convention of giving an "aside" with one hand held to partly cover the mouth, or by moving away briefly from the action in which he or she is engaged, or by speaking sotto voce. These asides are usually directed to the audience or to members of the cast other than the one to which the protagonist is speaking at the moment. As Goffman (1959) has observed, real life examples often occur between members of the same "team" who keep their team members informed about their actual thoughts and feelings while presenting another face to the audience or to their opposition.

(3) *Double*—An auxiliary player standing behind the protagonist to help express inner feelings. In a psychodrama, the person who will act as a "double" is encouraged to sit or stand in exactly the same position as the protagonist and to try to duplicate his or her bodily tension so that the double can more effectively resonate to unexpressed thoughts and feelings. As we have noted in the description of the functions of a chorus, doubling may be performed by a number of persons acting together. Real life examples occur in families when parents try to help children express thoughts or feelings, in groups where not everyone shares a common language and some people interpret for others, or in almost any setting when one person is

having difficulty communicating an idea and another begins: "What X is trying to say is...."

(4) *Mirror*—An auxiliary player presents the behavior of the protagonist, who steps out of the scene to observe. Parents often mimic their children's repeated requests for another glass of water at bedtime, and repeat other behaviors to indicate what they look like to other people. Teachers of mechanical skills, voice, or whatever, use the technique with their students to indicate what is being done wrong before demonstrating how it can be done right. Another example is impersonation, included by Benedetti (1976) in his list of highly dramatic real life situations.

(5) *Concretizing*—A visual depiction of feelings or relationships. In a psychodrama, if the protagonist indicates a feeling of being pulled in two or more directions by certain attractive alternatives, the director may ask several auxiliary players to represent the desired persons, objects, or ideas, and actually pull the protagonist in different directions at the same time. The protagonist may be asked to struggle with the auxiliaries until some let go. Again the family provides ready-made examples when two or more children attempt to move one parent in the direction of their desired activities.

(6) *Maximizing*—Increasing or exaggerating the emotional content of a communication or attitude. In a psychodrama, a protagonist may be asked to increase the intensity of an expression of emotion as an aid to reaching an emotional catharsis, in the hope that some insight may follow. For example, a protagonist who is angry may be instructed to beat a pillow to give vent to the anger. Or if a protagonist feels rejected, a group of auxiliary players may be instructed to shout terms of abuse or to turn their backs on the protagonist. In real life the maximizing is often initiated by the protagonist to increase the effect on the audience, as when one declares "You are breaking my heart," while clutching at one's chest and looking anguished. Children seem to use this technique quite naturally in their teasing chants of persons who have become scapegoats.

(7) *Empty chair*—An empty chair is used to represent a person, part of the self, value, or abstract symbol. In a psychodrama, chairs, cushions, or other objects are often placed in positions in the action area to represent the distance between the protagonist and other persons who are not present. Persons in any form of therapy sometimes find it easier to talk to an empty chair or an empty ceiling (if they are on a couch) than they would to talk directly to the therapist or the person involved. In everyday life, empty chairs are often left at the dining table to symbolize the absent guest. Sometimes whole rooms or even houses are kept furnished just as they were when they were occupied by some famous person or loved one so that others

can still come into their presence. A less somber version of the empty chair is used when students place "markers" such as books, sweaters, or sandwiches in sets of chairs at a university library table as an indication that the student's self extends into a territory beyond that occupied by the actual student.

Audience

An audience is crucial for the theatrical experience. As observers and critics of the theater point out, there is no play until it is performed (there is only a script), and there is no performance unless there is an audience. Thus the main difference between theater and ordinary life would seem to be that in theater, no matter how real or imagined are the relationships between the actors who mount the stage, their main intention is to transmit an "illusion" to an audience. For the most part, in everyday life, the persons involved really do have relations to each other and really do have a task to perform, whether an audience is present or not. To the extent that this difference between theater and everyday life holds, the analysis of theatrical activity and the use of theatrical concepts as metaphors should be most useful when the actions of everyday people are primarily intended to transmit an image to some onlooker and least useful when the primary goal of everyday persons is to cooperate in reaching some goal. As it turns out, at least from the symbolic interactionist point of view, there is a considerable overlap in the two kinds of activity because all cooperative tasks require the coordination of a set of roles. The coordination of roles depends upon the ways in which the roles are, and are seen to be, performed. Goffman (1959), in particular, has provided ample evidence of the preoccupation that a real life actor has in presenting himself or herself to an audience, even an audience of one.[2]

The distinction between theater that requires an audience and everyday life is eroded further if we consider that very often in everyday life there is an audience present and the actors are aware of it (examples will be given below) and that even in a small work or discussion group all members are not usually active at the same time. Although the presence of subgroups was not stressed in many of the early laboratory studies of group discussion, there were typically two or three persons who did most of the talking while the others sat back as members of the audience (Hare, 1982: 144-145). Even in a group of two, when a new image is presented, one person is in the role of protagonist, and the other a listener or member of the audience. It is only after the image has been presented that a complementary role can be assumed either in support of or against the image.

Real or Symbolic Events and Absence or Presence of Audience

Because we can expect that group members will pay more attention to the *meaning* of an activity if it is both symbolic and intended for an audience, and more attention to the *actual behavior* when the focus is on the completion of some actual task and there is no audience present, it should be possible to learn more about the effect of an audience if we arrange activities for comparison as suggested below:

Relationship to Audience	Nature of event (examples)	
	Real	Symbolic
no audience	family, work groups	meetings of cult members, fraternity initiations
provision for small audiences from time to time	kibbutzim or other experimental communities, industries that provide tours	rituals such as rainmaking
provision is made for audience	trials, weddings, amateur sports	religious observances performed by priests, medicine men, etc.
audience composed of persons who did not expect an enactment	crime in public places, terrorism	street theater
audience required for a performance	professional sports	stage plays, musical or dance shows, or other entertainments

Plot Development

The bare outlines of the plot are fairly simple, as Brockett (1964: 26-29) records: a plot has a beginning, a middle, and an end, including an obligatory scene when all the facts are revealed. Or using the metaphor of birth, Bentley (1967: 15) passes along the comment of an earlier French critic that "something is born, develops, and dies between the beginning and the end." Unless the entire play takes place in one act, there are usually several major subdivisions of the play. For each of these acts, ideally, the curtain fall should sum up the act and forecast the action in the next act (Hamilton, 1939: 64).

Within any act there may be two or more scenes. The characteristics of a scene as recorded by Van Laan (1970: 229) are the following:

(1) Any narrative unit, having its own beginning, middle, and end.
(2) Stands out in overall pattern of action as a self-contained sequence of incidents.
(3) Limitations may be a change of locale or a temporary clearing of the stage.
(4) In Greek tragedy, the odes or the chorus separate the scenes.
(5) There is a shift in focus.

All of these guidelines for the identification of acts and scenes can be used in the analysis of the phases in the development of everyday activity. As we will see in the examples of dramaturgical analysis given in the following chapters, the first step is often to make a time line on a piece of paper and note the natural divisions of the action into acts and scenes. On the stage all activity is compressed into a real time of three hours or less, whereas in everyday life, an act or scene may extend over a period of days or months, or it may be of only a few minutes duration. Whatever the occasion, time is an important variable and a limited amount of time is often the major source of stress during an event. This is especially obvious in cases of terrorist actions when hostages have been taken and the time set for their possible release approaches.

In the theater, as in real life, "time" not only refers to the passing of time but to the time of day, month, year, or century that the action takes place. Each of these times carries with it a set of expectations for the kind of action that can or cannot take place. Tension occurs because as Heathcote points out: "A drama is a trap into a particular time, place, and circumstance. This is the fixed moment, and there is no escaping it; it can only be worked through" (Wagner, 1979: 149).

Summary

The theatrical event may be likened to the symbolic voyage taken by the shaman to the "illud tempus," the place where creativity is always happening, and the return by the hungan who is possessed of the new inspiration and must now communicate it to an audience. The presentation of a new idea by an ordinary person in an ordinary group is similar in that any insight concerning the definition of the situation that the group is in or the task they face must first be conceptualized and then presented to the group as audience before roles can be taken that relate to the idea.

In the theater plays have been classified in four major types. Two are serious, melodrama and tragedy, involving heroes and villains, and two are expressive, farce and comedy, involving fools. Melodramas and farces are plot driven whereas tragedies and comedies are dependent on characterization. Polti concluded that all plays were combinations of 36 dramatic situations. However these 36 can in turn be grouped into seven sets according to system level and the principal dimension of interaction that forms the basis of the plot.

Just as social psychologists have been concerned with whether or not "drama" should be used as a metaphor for describing social reality or is actually the way things are, so persons involved with the theater have also been concerned with the relationship between theater and life. They conclude that the same elements are present in both situations but that theater intensifies life experiences. Contemporary theater companies attempt to eliminate any distinction between theater and life by having their actors move to the street and take part in meaningful symbolic or actual behavior.

Descriptions of theater activity by directors, actors, and critics provide a set of hypotheses concerning the expected impact of staging on social action, in terms of the "scene/act" ratio, and the expected behaviors of persons who play the real life roles of playwrights, directors, actors (protagonists, auxiliaries, and members of the chorus), and members of the audience. Techniques used by actors onstage and in psychodramas in presenting images can also be identified in everyday activity. The techniques include the following: role reversal, soliloquy, double, mirror, concretizing, maximizing, and the empty chair.

All forms of collective behavior from everyday events through theatrical performances can be classified along a continuum according to their relationship to an audience and according to whether the behavior is intended to be real or symbolic.

For the analysis of plot development one can use a time line and denote the beginnings and endings of acts and scenes. If the amount of time available for a real life drama is short, it may be a major source of stress. The time required for the adequate development of an idea by a group may vary from a few minutes to a lifetime.

Notes

1. The commanding image is presumably a reflection of the essence that Clark (1971: 3) refers to as the subtext: "that vast and powerful meaning that swirls beneath the apparently logical order of the words in the text."

2. Using Goffman's approach Messinger, Sampson, and Towne (1962) provide additional evidence from observations in a mental hospital where patients attempt to project a normal "self," only to worry later whether they are really normal or not.

PART II

APPLICATIONS FROM CONFLICT AND CONFLICT RESOLUTION

Find the truthful core in views of every kind.
—Dom Helder Camara, 1974

Chapter 3

Protest Demonstrations in South Africa and Curacao

In this chapter, we begin our application of some of the aspects of the dramaturgical perspective with the examination of the levels of creativity, types of images, and stages in development in three instances of conflict between protestors and police. Two of the confrontations happened in South Africa, one at Sharpeville in 1960 and another at the Rand Mines in 1975.[1] The third case is from Curacao in 1969. In the case of the Rand Mines, there is also an example of successful resolution of conflict. The case is included here rather than in Chapter 5 where the emphasis is on conflict resolution so that it is possible to compare an unsuccessful and a successful intervention of third parties.

As an introduction to these cases, we will first note some of the main groups and subgroups that are typically involved in confrontations in South Africa and some of the areas of conflict between and within groups. The case of Sharpeville provides an example of the problems that can occur when subgroups within the police force and within the group of protestors have different motivations and different styles of behavior.

Areas of Conflict Between and Within Groups

The collection of case studies entitled *The Struggle for Democracy in South Africa* (Hare, 1983b) provides a set of descriptions of instances of conflict and attempts at conflict resolution during the period 1977-1981. Three of the cases in that volume involve squatters and government representatives, two cases are boycotts, one of buses and one of schools, and three cases involve disputes between labor and management. In the course of the analysis, four areas of conflict are identified that occur in almost every case. These areas of conflict are illustrated in Figure 3.1 (Hare, 1983b: 147). The small square in the upper left section of Figure 3.1 represents the predominantly white management or government. Inside this square are two smaller boxes to indicate the possibility of differences of opinion between two or more branches of the South African Government or between the South African Government and a homeland government or between different branches of management. The large square in the lower right represents the predominantly black protestors, be they squatters, commuters, scholars, or workers. Inside the square are two smaller boxes representing some of the subgroups that may be present, for example the "conservatives" and the "progressives." Within one of the smaller boxes are small circles to indicate the various leader and follower roles that must be played in the group. The double-headed arrows at different points in the figure indicate points at which conflicts of interest may arise.

Although when the analysis of the cases was begun, the primary interest was in the conflicts between the white group—represented by the small upper square—and the protesting black group—represented by the large lower square—in every case, differences of approach were discovered within the black protest group that either made it difficult to reach agreement with the white establishment or significantly altered the course of events. In some cases, there were also differences of opinion between some of the leaders who had been detained in prison and some of their more progressive supporters who were still outside and had taken over the leadership. Finally, different branches of government or management did not always agree. Thus, although there were problems requiring some form of conflict resolution between establishment and protest groups with widely different

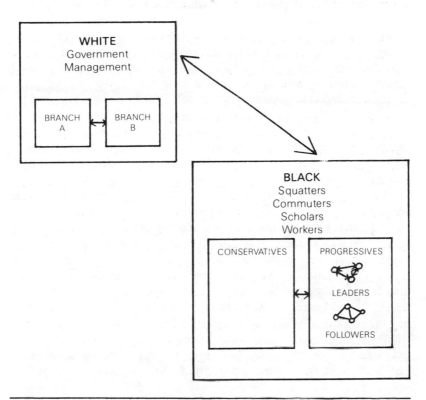

Figure 3.1   Four Areas of Potential Conflict

levels of resources in terms of economic and political power, there were also conflicts of interest between groups of roughly equal status.

Sharpeville, 1960

For the analysis of any incident of conflict or conflict resolution, it is best if the persons recording the event are familiar with the theoretical categories that will be used in the analysis. When this is the case, they can record relevant information that may well be overlooked by an observer with a more general orientation. However, in the case of the incident at the Sharpeville police station on Monday, March 21, 1960, there is no evidence that any social scientist was present, least of all one using a "dramaturgical perspective." However, Judge Wessels, who was appointed as a commission to investigate and report on these events, provided a report of some 200 pages that gives the background of the occurrences as well as an hour-by-hour account of the activities during the morning and early afternoon (Wessels, 1960). The references to the Commission report are to paragraph numbers rather than page numbers, because I was using an English translation of the official report (that was only issued in Afrikaans) and the page numbers may not be the same.

The events at Sharpeville were only one part of a nationwide protest organized by members of the Pan Africanist Congress in the hope that if a sufficient number of persons without passes would present themselves for arrest at police stations then the ensuing work stoppage would signal the beginning of a major protest on the part of blacks. The leaders of the P.A.C. hoped that in three-years time the country would be turned over to them. During the weekend before March 21, and in the early hours of that Monday morning, there had been confrontations between police and groups of black protestors. Some of these confrontations had been violent, and large crowds had gathered, especially on Seeiso Street, not far from the Sharpeville police station. During the night, the telephone lines to the police station had been cut, so that there was no direct communication with police at the station about the conditions there until police vehicles with radios arrived later in the day. Thus, unfortunately for the persons who eventually gathered in the crowd at the Sharpeville police station, impressions were formed about their behavior by some of the key police officers that were based on information about conflicts that had occurred at other locations earlier in the day.

The main activity began at the Sharpeville police station at 8:00 a.m. when Tsolo, a 20-year-old leader of the P.A.C., arrived with a group of about 40 blacks and asked that they be arrested because they were not carrying passes. Sergeant Nkosi said that he could not arrest anyone and that they must wait for one of the white officers to arrive. At 9:00 a.m., Head Constable Heyl arrived and took over command. This followed the custom of the police that whenever an officer of higher rank arrived on the scene, he would be given command. As a result, the command at the Sharpeville police station changed four times during the morning and early afternoon, about every hour or hour-and-a-half, and no officer in charge was able to form a direct impression of the mood of the crowd over the whole period.

When Head Constable Heyl arrived, Tsolo again asked that his group be arrested. He was told to make his representations to the government and not to the police. By this time, the crowd around the police station was estimated to be more than 3,000 persons. At 10:30 a.m., Lt. Visser (a member of the detective branch) took over command. Tsolo again asked to be locked up. After his conversations with Lt. Visser the impression was given to the crowd that some important official would come to speak to them at 2:00 p.m. From then on, many members of the crowd were simply waiting or watching the events unfold as airplanes buzzed the area in an attempt to disperse the crowd, but only succeeding in attracting more interest. From time to time, various groups of police reinforcements with vehicles arrived and passed through the crowd and into the police station through the front double gate (see Figure 3.2). At 11:30 a.m., a group of police took up a position outside the fence surrounding the police station at the entrance of Zwane Street. Although they observed the shooting that took place later, they did not take part in it. During this period, Tsolo and two other leaders were able to control the crowd when they were asked by police to do so (Wessels: para. 183). By this time, a group of curious onlookers had formed along the front section of the fence. On occasion, the fence was bent inward as they pressed forward to see the latest arrivals of police.

At 11:20 a.m., Captain Theron arrived with more police and took over command. He regarded the position as serious and decided to disperse the crowd. He radioed for reinforcements (Wessels: para. 191). About this time, Tsolo had gone off for something to eat. Twelve bottles of cool drink were brought to the police by members of the crowd. The police, who regarded the gift as a taunt, asked that the bottles be removed (Wessels: para. 192). By 1:00 p.m., more security police and three armored cars had arrived, bringing the total number of armored cars inside the fence to four (Wessels: para. 193). A group of youths just outside the gate at the front of the police station taunted and threatened the police (Wessels: para. 195).

At 1:00 p.m., Lt. Colonel Spengler, of the Security Branch, had arrived. He decided that it might have a beneficial effect on the crowd

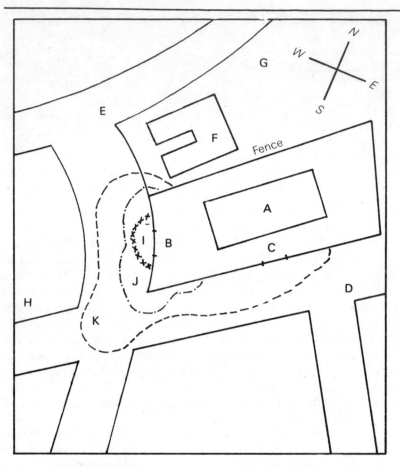

A – Police station   G – North field
B – Main entrance   H – Clinic
C – Side entrance   I – Hostile youths
D – Zwane Street   J – Curious onlookers
E – Seeiso Street   K – Main crowd
F – Cafes and shops

NOTE: Sketch from photographs in Reeves, 1960.

Figure 3.2   Sharpeville Police Station and Position of Crowd

if he took their leaders inside the police station. So he took Tsolo inside to question him and kept him there (Wessels: para. 197).

Between 1:10 and 1:20 p.m., Lt. Colonel Pienaar drove through the crowd to take command. As he approached the gate, some people struck his car with sticks and he urged his driver to speed through (Wessels: para. 202). Before his arrival, he had been briefed by Major van Zyl about some of the conflicts that had occurred earlier in the day at other locations where there had been violence and attempts to disperse the crowd. Unfortunately, "it is quite clear that Pienaar was under the impression that the attempt to disperse the crowd had taken place at the police station" (Wessels: para. 201). Lt. Col. Pienaar's emotional state at the time is indicated in his statement to the Commission (Wessels: para. 204):

> When I landed inside that yard that morning, from all I had seen and been told and what I had personally experienced, I was satisfied that the mob was ready for anything. The mob was in a frenzied state and I feared an attack on the police at any moment.

In contrast to Lt. Col. Pienaar's impression, the Commission found "no acceptable evidence of any common purpose to attack the police" and the fact that Lt. Col. Spengler considered it safe to open the double gate to take some of the leaders to the police station shows that the members of the Security Branch were not expecting an immediate attack (Wessels: para. 225).

However, Lt. Col. Pienaar's definition of the situation prevailed. As he testified to the Commission (Wessels: para. 229):

> I have had 36 years of service and I have dealt with many mobs. I know what the psychology of a mob is. They have no conscience, are capable of any rash act, and when I landed in the yard, there, my first concern was to muster the police and to form them up in readiness for any possible attack that might come.

Lt. Col. Pienaar then ordered 70 policemen to line up about 7 or 8 paces from the fence facing the crowd in front of the police station. He gave the order to load five rounds.

After the police had been lined up, Lt. Col. Spengler went outside the double gate with the intention of detaining a man in a red shirt who was making a lot of noise. This man did not come in but another man came forward and said that he wished to surrender himself (Wessels: para. 242). There was some sort of brief struggle, some members of the crowd appeared to be coming through the open gate, and the police began to fire although no order had been given. At first, in the confusion, some members of the crowd in the back continued to press forward to see, but within seconds most had turned and started to run away. The police firing probably lasted no more than 20-30 seconds (Wessels: para. 283) before Lt. Col. Pienaar and other officers were able to bring it under control by jumping in front of the policemen, shouting "stop" and waving their hands (Wessels: para. 284). The time was now 1:40 p.m.

There were 130 white and 77 black policemen inside the fence. Another 29 white and 62 black policemen were outside the fence. They were ordered not to fire. By the time the shooting stopped, 75 policemen had fired about 700 shots killing 69 and wounding 180 members of the crowd (Wessels: para. 81). About 70% of those killed or wounded had been shot in the back (Wessels: para. 269). It took about one hour to remove the dead and injured (Wessels: para. 310). Judge Wessels (para. 311) concluded that "nothing of note happened later in the day."

A Dramaturgical Analysis of the Events at Sharpeville

For the dramaturgical analysis of an event, two types of diagrams are useful. One is a variation of the "field diagram" proposed by Bales that indicates the relative positions of the actors or images in the four-dimensional space (upward-downward, positive-negative, serious-expressive, and conforming-anticonforming (see Figure 3.3). The other diagram depicts the variations over time in the amount of involvement and creativity of the main individual and group theme carriers during the course of the action (see Figure 3.4).

Depending upon the amount of detail one wishes to record, one might draw field diagrams to indicate the position of actors or images as during each "scene" or "act" in the course of the development of the action. However, in the case of Sharpeville, one field diagram may suffice to indicate the positions of the images that crowd members and police had of themselves and each other at the time the police fired. According to the testimony before the Commission, members of the crowd suggested that although songs were sung and slogans

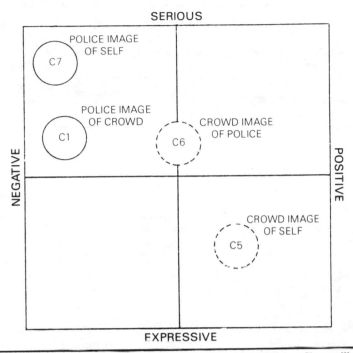

Figure 3.3   Field Diagram of Images Held by Crowd and Police at Sharpeville

shouted "the crowd was good-humoured throughout." Whereas in the police view "those present at the police station had already been involved earlier in the day in incidents where violence was used both against and by the police; that the feelings of the crowd at the police station gradually became charged through incitement by the leaders until breaking point was reached when at about 1:40 p.m. they started to attack the police and that the police were then obliged to shoot in order to ward off the attack" (Wessels: para. 82).

In Figure 3.3, the images held by members of the crowd are indicated by dashed circles. They see themselves as active (upward) but not too dominant, positive, expressive, and conforming (waiting for someone to speak to them). The images held by members of the police are indicated by the two circles in the upper lefthand corner. The police see the crowd as violent (upward and negative), serious, and anticon-

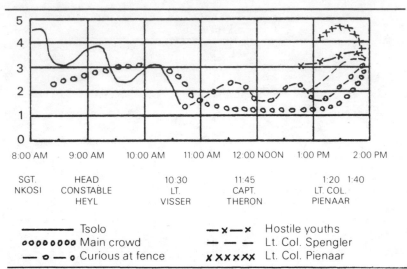

Figure 3.4   Involvement and Creativity of Theme Carriers at Sharpeville Police Station

forming. In order to control the crowd, the police felt it was necessary to be even more upward, negative, serious, and conforming, in order to drive them back. Unfortunately for the members of the crowd, the events in other areas on the previous night and morning, where some of the police had been on duty, served to remind them of the violence that had occurred at Cato Manor (Wessels: para. 211). There, on January 24, 1960, four white and five black policemen had been murdered by members of a drunken crowd during a weekend liquor raid by the police (Ladlau, 1975: 92-97).

A diagram depicting the variations over time of the involvement and creativity of the main theme carriers is given in Figure 3.4. At the left of the diagram is a scale representing the levels of involvement (from 0 to 5) as they are coded according to the previously defined categories for involvement/creativity. At the bottom of the figure is a time line marking each hour and half hour from 8:00 a.m. until 2:00 p.m. on Monday, March 21, 1960. The times that the different police officers took command and the time the shooting started is also indicated. The action begins at 8:00 a.m. with Tsolo and the group of about 40 blacks asking to be put in prison. Their initiative (coded as level 5) defined the initial situation at the police station to which Sgt. Nkosi responded. The creativity of Tsolo and his group drops and then rises briefly as they repeat their request to Head Constable Heyl at 9:00 a.m., and later to Lt. Visser. After 10:30, we do not hear about Tsolo's group again.

The involvement of the main crowd (indicated by small circles) begins at about level 2 as they gather to see what is happening. Their level of involvement rises to about level 3 at about 10:30 a.m. when they accept the definition of the situation that someone important will come to speak to them about 2:00 p.m. in the afternoon. They then settle down to wait until 1:40 p.m. when they suddenly discover that they are under attack and flee. Within the main crowd, two smaller segments can be identified. One group consists of the curious onlookers (graph indicated by circles and dashes) who press against the fence from time to time when new police arrive or when Lt. Col. Spengler goes outside the fence to detain someone. The other group contains the hostile youths (graph indicated by crosses and dashes) who gather near the fence and taunt the police. It is the action of these two smaller segments of the crowd that make the major contribution to the image that the police form of the whole crowd, as it is the pressure from the curious at the fence and the stones thrown by the hostile youth that set off the police firing.

However, it is clear that the major theme carrier at the event was Lt. Col. Pienaar who arrived on the scene already convinced that he had only one course of action that might avoid a "blood bath." Without even taking time to order the crowd to disperse he lined up his men and ordered them to load their guns. Thus when Lt. Col. Spengler decided to go outside the gate to detain the last leader, he set in motion a fast-moving sequence of action and reaction that served to convince the other police that their definition of the situation was correct. A few seconds after 1:40 p.m. the creativity on the part of all the actors fell away abruptly, on the police side there was "apparently a feeling of despondency about what had happened" (Wessels: para. 306).

For a single case, such as Sharpeville, one of the main values of using any theory, in this instance a dramaturgical perspective, is that the analyst is forced to consider systematically how the various aspects of the action fit together in terms of the theory. The result, for the single case, may seem to be much as if the case had only been described again but using a different set of terms that one might use in a newspaper report, or the report of a Commission. The advantages of a theory become more evident when two or more cases are systematically compared, as we will do in the next section concerned with conflicts in the Rand Mines in 1975.

Rand Mines 1975

In 1975, a series of protests swept through mines on the Rand that employed workers from Lesotho. It was no coincidence as the miners were all complaining about the same action by the Lesotho Government, and the miners in different mines were in direct communication with each other. Although the initial circumstances were approximately the same in each mine, the actions of the mine management varied considerably from one mine to the next. As a result, in some mines there were fights between sets of miners, between miners and police, damage to property, injuries and deaths, and many miners sent home. At the other end of the continuum, the management of one mine acted as a third party to help the miners solve the problem. There were no disruptions on that mine. As an indication of some of the processes of conflict and conflict resolution that were at work, cases at each end of the continuum are contrasted in terms of a dramaturgical analysis of the creativity of each of the groups involved.

Horner and Kooy (1980: 9ff.) provide a brief background and description of the events in the mines as follows:

> In November 1974 the Lesotho Government promulgated regulations making compulsory the deferment of 60 per cent of the monthly pay of Lesotho nationals into the Lesotho National Bank, to be refunded to the miner on his return to Lesotho after the completion of his contract. Voluntary deferred pay schemes had been operating for miners from Botswana, Lesotho, Swaziland, and South Africa since 1918, administered by the Native Recruiting Corporation, and at the time of the introduction of the new regulations, about 80 per cent of Lesotho nationals had been subscribing voluntarily to the scheme. A compulsory scheme for Mozambicans had operated for many years without overt worker resistance and a similar scheme was later introduced for Malawians.

> It is possible that some of the detail of the new scheme was misunderstood by the Basotho workers, but they understood that the Lesotho

regime would be using their money and they objected strongly. The majority of Lesotho nationals on the mines were opposed to the government of Chief Jonathan and suspected that their money would be used by the Bank of Lesotho to meet the needs of the government.

In January 1975 there were seven incidents revolving around the deferred pay scheme, involving Basotho miners in large numbers. Basotho workers stood solidly together on this issue and on at least four mines almost the entire Basotho work force took part in the strikes. They picketed in an attempt to engage the support of other workers; it seems that they were successful in some but not with others and on some occasions attempts to stop other miners going on shift developed into violence.

At least 8,500 Basotho and Tswana miners left the mines and went home. . . . During the disturbances mine property, including kitchens, liquor outlets, a recreation hall and shaft-head buildings, were damaged, and mine management and indunas were attacked.

In their overall pattern, the protests proceeded through eight stages (acts):

(1) Mine management learns of the change in withholding pay introduced by the homeland government.
(2) Management informs some or all of the workers involved.
(3) The national group involved stages a protest.
(4) There is conflict with other groups of miners.
(5) The South African police are called, and respond.
(6) During a period of quiet, meetings are held.
(7) The kitchen or liquor outlet is looted.
(8) Up to several thousand miners request to return home and are discharged.

The amount of overt conflict varied from mine to mine.[2] For analysis, two contrasting cases have been selected. In one, with the least creative reaction on the part of management, the police were called to intervene on several occasions, using tear gas and small arms. By the end of the incident—which included three days of overt conflict—seven miners were dead and twenty-six injured. Damage to the hostel amounted to approximately 7,000 dollars. Management discharged 2,994 miners. In the case with the most creative response on the part of management, a delegation of miners was formed with the support of management. The delegation traveled by bus to their homeland capital. In an interview with the Minister of Finance, they were able to secure more favorable withholding conditions concerning their pay. Miners of the same nationality in all the mines then received the same benefit.

Because protests over working conditions have occurred from time to time in South African mines, the variety of forms that a protest might take would be known to those who initiate the protest. Thus the initial idea of the miners is in the nature of a "theme." They know the general direction of their own action and the general goal that they wish to reach, but the way the action develops will depend very much upon the reactions of the counter-players: management, other miners, and police. All of these key roles are out of their control.

In these cases, the protests in the mines took place within a period of approximately two and a half weeks from the time the management informed some or all of the miners and the time the protest was concluded. For a visual representation of the group activity in the mines that represent the two contrasting cases, one can plot the action of each group involved with time as the horizontal axis and the five levels of creativity as the vertical axis (see Figure 3.5). As each group reaches a peak of activity, at whatever level, one can note the ratings on the four dimensions that characterize the social-emotional process. This type of rating for groups is similar to the type of rating of "images" proposed by Bales and Cohen for the analysis of individual behavior in small groups (Bales and Cohen, 1979).

In Figure 3.5, in the case of the least creative mine management (upper graph), we see the management as a small group in the role of director operating at about Level 2 during the first three days as they notify the senior blacks of the affected national group about the new withholding scheme. These senior blacks are employed, in the roles of auxiliaries, to assist in the administration of the hostels. They are instructed not to make public announcements, but only to respond to questions if asked. They act accordingly, reaching a "peak" of activity at about Level 2, over a period of three days. The activity of the managers and the senior blacks over the first five days constitutes the first act of this drama, that of notification.

By the fifth day, the members of the dance team (a relatively youthful group of men who perform traditional dances on festive occasions) begin to take over the leadership as protagonists or "theme

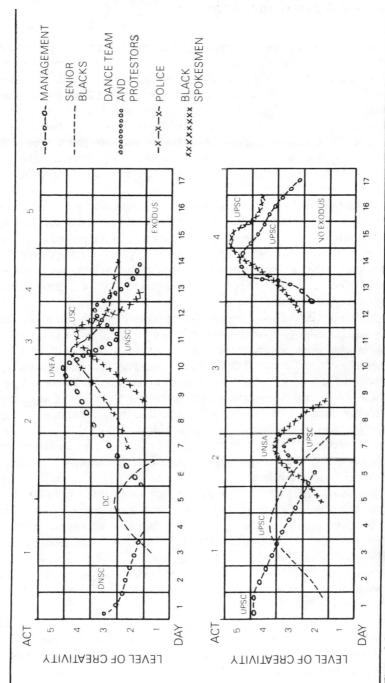

Figure 3.5 Level of Creativity and Social-Emotional Behavior of Groups in Two Mine Incidents

carriers" for the miners. Their protest activity, that provides the main definition of the situation for all parties, reaches a peak on the tenth day at Level 4, as the police (antagonists) intervene for the first time. The police have been called by the management. Act 2 consists of this initial confrontation between protestors and police.

Act 3 begins on the eleventh day as the activity of the dance team drops to Level 2 when spokesmen for the miners (who are team leaders underground) take the initiative as the new protagonists to try to find a solution for the conflict. The activity of the team leaders reaches a peak at Level 4.

Act 4 begins on the twelfth day with another confrontation between the protestors and the police. The activity of the dance team rises to Level 3. However their theme leadership ends as the police disperse the protest and there is a general exodus from the mines (act 5). Throughout the incident once the protest had begun, the various groups of miners maintained the initiative and the management and the police responded.

Going back over the graph for the least creative situation, we can now add the ratings of social-emotional process in terms of the four dimensions of behavior. Although ratings could be made for each "scene" or "act" in the drama, they are given here only when the creativity for a group reaches a peak as an indication of the overall direction of the social-emotional movement. First, as the management briefs the senior blacks, the management's activity is rated as downward (submissive)-negative-serious-conforming (DNSC) as they appear to be taking the minimum amount of initiative in informing their workers of the change in the conditions of their pay. The senior blacks also give a minimal response and are rated as downward-conforming (DC), that is "neutral" ratings are given on the positive-negative and serious-expressive dimensions. As the theme carrier for the protesting miners the dance team is rated upward-negative-expressive-anti(non)conforming (UNEA) as they channel the hostile feelings of the miners towards other workers, the police, and the management. The black team leaders who briefly take over as spokesmen for the miners are rated as upward-serious-conforming (USC). As Leary (1957) has noted for individuals, the activity of theme carriers in different parts of the social-emotional space (here described in terms of four dimensions) tends to "pull" certain behavior from other persons (or groups) who occupy other positions in the space. Thus, for example, the UNEA behavior of the dance team is quite likely to pull upward-negative-serious-conforming behavior from the police. In contrast the upward-serious-conforming behavior of the team leaders will not appear to be as threatening to the authorities.

In these graphs, the activity of the majority of the miners who took roles as members of the audience, or chorus, or auxiliaries has not been included as there was not enough detail in the available accounts. When the dramaturgical perspective is used in direct observation, the activities of all of the principal actors and groups can be recorded, although for events such as these, involving a large number of people, a team of observers would be needed.

Turning now to the case of the most creative mine management (lower graph), the graph begins on the first day with the activity of management at Level 4. The managers, acting in the roles of directors, not only brief their senior blacks but also instruct them to pass the word to all concerned. The senior blacks, as auxiliaries, respond actively in informing the workers, reaching a peak at Level 3 on the fourth day. The first act of notification ends on the fifth day. Act 2 begins on the sixth day as some of the black team leaders from underground come forward as spokesmen (protagonists) for the miners, reaching a peak at Level 3 as they agree with management to wait until the return of one of the mine management officials who has gone to the homeland capital to see if there is anything that can be done to change the directive concerning pay. Act 3 consists of a period of waiting, days eight through twelve. Act 4 begins on the thirteenth day after the management's representative has failed to secure any concession from the homeland government. The black team leaders again take the role of protagonists as they form a twenty-six man delegation to visit the homeland capital (Level 5). The suggestion of a delegation was actually put forward by management who then arranged for a bus and sent along one member of management to facilitate the border crossing. The management representative did not actually attend the meeting with the homeland Finance Minister. However the supporting activity of management, now acting as an auxiliary, is rated as Level 4. The miners' delegation secured a favorable concession from the Finance Minister and returned joyfully to the mine. The police did not intervene, there was no damage to persons or property, and no exodus from the mine.

In terms of the four dimensions of social-emotional behavior, the initial activity of management in informing the miners is rated UPSC and the response of the senior blacks is also UPSC. The initial activity of the team leader spokesmen was UNSA as they presented the miners' case. They were won over by the arguments and the UPSC behavior of management. At the time of the visit to the homeland, both the delegation and the supporting group of management were UPSC.

During the course of the protest, some of the groups involved played a consistent role, some varied their role, and in the case of the ad hoc delegation of miners, one new group was formed and then disbanded once the protest was over. The consistency of the role of each group can be analyzed in terms of the three aspects of group behavior: form (structure), process, and content (function). The most consistent were the South African police who maintained the same structure, process, and function throughout (enforcing the norms, or I). Next was the dance team, in the case with the least creative management, that has the same structure and function (stating a value position, or L) but changed its process. That is, during normal periods the function of the dance team is to represent the traditional values of the society through dance. The members of the dance team could be expected to be especially sensitive to underlying cultural themes and to their expression in bodily movement. Thus their usual process involving UPEC behavior in the traditional dance became UNEA as they became the theme carriers for the protest. In some of the other mines, both the dance team and the football (soccer) team played similar roles. Again it is easy to see how a football team can become the expression of the spirit of a national group at a time of protest in the same way that they represent their national group on the sports field.

During the protest, the management in the most creative case kept the same structure but changed their function and their process as they played a third-party role to help secure some relief from the problem that faced the miners (moving from their ordinary position of leadership, or G, to one of conflict resolution, or I). Finally the ad hoc group of delegates was entirely new in its structure, process, and function (I).

The dramaturgical analysis given above was presented at a workshop for personnel managers from some of the mines involved where the objective was to draw up new guidelines to deal with "unrest." Noting that even in the case of the most creative mine management an "ad hoc" group had to be formed before the crisis could be met, it was suggested that at times of crisis a third-party group, or network of individuals, be formed with representatives from all groups that might be involved to search for constructive creative solutions (Hare, 1982: 155-180). Although this suggestion has not yet been taken up, management have included in their new guidelines the recommendation that the miners be encouraged to hold their demonstration and meeting with mine management on the sports field away from the mine offices. By moving the "stage" away from the front of the mine offices, members of management who are backstage will have more time and be under less direct pressure when they search for a solution to the problem.

Curacao, May 30, 1969

The riot on the island of Curacao, Netherlands Antilles, on May 30, 1969, provides an example of the developmental stages of functional theory at the general and more specific levels. As in so many colonial situations, the social and political stratification of the island followed racial lines. Over 95% of the island's population were black, a reminder that this was the largest slave port in the Caribbean at one time. The governor was from Holland and the marines who were flown from Holland to put down the riot were also Dutch because the Netherlands Antilles did not have its own army. Government officials and school teachers were usually immigrants or contract laborers from Holland. The business community that catered to a large tourist trade was composed mainly of Sephardic Jews who were encouraged by the Dutch to play this role from the times of the early settlement. Perhaps the only unusual feature in the class structure was that the bottom of the hierarchy was given over to the Portuguese, who swept the streets and sold ice cream—two types of work that even the lowest class of blacks avoided. Thus any disturbance was likely to break along racial lines.

During the period preceding the riot there had been a significant amount of unemployment as the Shell Oil refinery, which dominated the island's industry, had cut back on its labor force as an adjustment to changing markets and technology. This added the element of strain to the existing structural cleavages. Both of these factors influenced the general definition of the situation—L in functional terms (see Appendix 2 for Smelser's, 1962, analysis using these terms).

The precipitating events (I) consisted of a series of strikes called when labor negotiations appeared to be ineffective. These followed the general anxiety (A) concerning an adequate wage scale. The stage of mobilization (G) took the form of a march from one of the main gates of the Shell refinery to the center of the city of Willemstad with the intention of asking the Governor to intercede.

Although the overall course of events up to May 30th seems to fit Smelser's (1962) model and to have occurred in the expected order, the added value of a particular hypothesis concerning phases in development (i.e., L-A-I-G-L) is more evident in the analysis of the events during the day of May 30th. The data for this analysis come from a Dutch Government Commission report, a novel, pamphlets, press clippings, and interviews with participants. In brief, approximately 1,000 workers had assembled at Post (Gate) 5 of Shell at 7:30 a.m. at the changing of the shift. Various union leaders spoke, including "Poppa" Godet, a popular figure, who urged the group to follow him to town to ask for the intervention of the government in settling the strike. He said that if they did not obtain their goal without brute force, they would use it; thus the march clearly had the potential of becoming a hostile outburst. This speech gave meaning to the day's activity (L). As the march proceeded toward town, most of the marchers stayed in line. However, a few broke away to set fire to a car and to loot a shop, especially of its liquor supplies. From the hindsight of later events, this phase appears to be the educational phase (A) where group members learned about the "skills" that they would later use in their task. As the marchers came to the crest of a hill on the edge of town, they were stopped by police. During this confrontation "Poppa" Godet was shot. Although not seriously injured, he was taken to the hospital for treatment. This was the "precipitating factor" that changed the group structure (I) and also the specific group task (G). Looking back to the beginning of the day, we can see that the idea that there should be some form of protest (L), and the knowledge and experience of burning and looting (A) could have been organized in several ways. "Poppa" Godet had suggested one form of organization, a mass march, with himself in the lead. When his central leadership was removed during the police intervention (the person who fired the shot was never identified), the group did not need to go back to the L and A stages, but only to find a new structure (I) and with it a new specification of the task (G). Because the police were blocking the road so that the large mass of marchers (approximately 5,000 by this time) could not pass, the marchers broke into small groups, bypassed the police and swarmed down into the city to begin burning and looting the shops, primarily those of the Jewish merchants. This had the effect of providing a "short cut" to the redistribution of wealth that had been sought through wage negotiations.

Although Smelser discusses some aspects of the control of hostile outbursts (1962: 261 ff.), he gives only examples of military or police intervention and does not relate the interventions to particular phases in the development of the outbursts. In the Curacao example, we see the police intervene when the group is approaching their goal. The effect is to create a new "I" stage, and in this case to generate a new form of organization involving many small groups that the police are unable to handle.

Summary

Examples of protest demonstrations are drawn from Sharpeville in 1960 and Rand Mines in 1975, in South Africa, and Curacao, Netherlands Antilles in 1969. For dramaturgical analysis, three types of diagrams are found to be useful: (1) field diagrams that indicate the positions of the actions or images in a four-dimensional space, (2) diagrams indicating the involvement and creativity of actors on a five-point scale over time, and (3) diagrams that show the actors and audience in relation to the stage. For some events, an analysis in terms of the functional AGIL categories is also applied. Although most analyses of protest focus on the conflict between the protestors and the government or management officials who oppose them, there are also conflicts of interest within groups that should be considered in a more detailed description.

At Sharpeville in 1960, police and protestors differed in their images of each other. Unfortunately for the protestors, the police definition of the situation prevailed and the police fired on the crowd, killing and wounding many.

Protests in two different mines on the Rand in 1975 are described. In one, with a successful outcome, management made creative suggestions that were followed by an ad hoc group of mine workers' team leaders. In the other mine, the initiative was left to the protestors, led by the dance team, who launched the action, and to the police who were called in to stop it. The police restored control, but not without the deaths of some miners, damage to property, and an exodus of thousands of workers from the mine.

An analysis of the protest and riot on Curacao in 1969 using the AGIL functional categories shows how the dispersal of a group of protestors by police initiated a new integrative stage. Instead of being one line of protest marchers, the large group of unemployed workers split into many smaller groups that then evaded the police and swarmed down into the town to loot the stores.

Notes

1. An earlier version of the description of the protest in Sharpeville appeared in Hare (1980). The article also includes a typology for the analysis of protest groups according to whether the target of the protest is specific or diffuse and the initial style of behavior, nonviolent or violent. Eight stages that occurred in confrontations between protestors and police are identified with an example from a protest at Alexander Sinton High School in Cape Town.

2. The demonstrations usually took place within the hostels where between 5,000 and 7,000 men were housed.

Chapter 4

Greek and
Turkish Cypriots

We begin the chapter with a brief discussion of the part played by creativity in resolving social conflicts. In terms of dramaturgical analysis, the resolution takes the form of finding images, themes, plots, or scripts on which all parties can agree. This discussion is followed by a description of some of the activities of the "Cyprus Resettlement Project," when a transnational team helped Greek and Turkish Cypriots cooperate in solving a problem of common concern.

Conflict Resolution and Creativity

Some researchers concerned with finding the best solutions to social problems, especially those of a political nature, have emphasized the need for a creative problem-solving approach. Mary Parker Follett was an early advocate of the method in her book *Creative Experience* (1924). In solving the various social and political problems that she faced, she looked for solutions in which all parties would gain, usually through the introduction of some entirely new way of looking at the problem. She noted that "compromise between the old ways, or even combining the old ways, keep us always with . . . the old" (Follett, 1924: 160). Her enthusiasm is evident in the statement that "the act of co-creating is the core of democracy, the essence of citizenship, the condition of world citizenship" (Follett, 1924: 302).

Yet, many academics and practitioners involved in social conflict over the years seem not to have heard Follett's call. Half a century later, Deutsch reached a similar conclusion about the value of creative problem-solving. After reviewing his own and others' research on cooperation and competition, he observed that "apart from the writings of people connected with the nonviolence movement, little attempt has been made to distinguish between conflicts that achieve change through a process that is mutually rewarding to the parties involved in the conflict and one that is not. Yet change can take place either through a process of confrontation, which is costly to the conflicting groups, or it can take place through a process of problem solving, which is mutually rewarding to the conflicting groups" (Deutsch, 1973: 359).

Fisher and Ury (1978) divide their book on international mediation into three parts, each with a focus on a different problem. The problems are the following: (1) the human problem, (2) the inventing problem, and (3) the procedural problem. A solution to the "inventing problem" is the key to the whole process. Although it is helpful to have people who can get along well enough to work together (a solution to the human problem) and to have procedures that will maximize their ability to make decisions and solve problems (a solution to procedural problem), unless someone invents a creative solution the conflict will not be satisfactorily solved. Burton (1979) also cites cases in which solutions to major national and international conflicts required a whole new way of looking at the problem. On the other hand, Janis (1982) records a number of cases in which a process that he identifies as "group think" led to a fiasco as a result of a policy decision that did not use the creative potential of the group members.

Although most descriptions of creative problem-solving do not classify the "hypotheses" or "alternative solutions" according to the level of creativity involved, the levels of creativity identified by Taylor (1975: 306-308) can be used for this purpose (see Chapter 1).

Chronology of Cyprus Resettlement Project[1]

The Cyprus Resettlement Project, in operation from 1972 through 1974, was a peacemaking action in the image of the World Peace Brigade, a group founded in 1962 and dedicated to nonviolent action either as partisans on behalf of some oppressed people or as nonpartisans acting as mediators between conflicting groups. Like the "six characters in search of an author" the persons who initiated the

Cyprus Resettlement Project knew the roles they wished to play but needed a stage and a plot for their enactment.

The members of the World Peace Brigade carried out three actions between 1962 and 1966: the intervention on behalf of Zambian independence, 1962-1964 (Walker, 1977; Hare and Blumberg, 1980: 138-150), the Delhi-Peking March in 1963, and the third-party group monitoring the cease fire in Nagaland, 1964-1966 (Aram, 1977; Hare and Blumberg, 1980: 151-168). After 1966, there had been no meetings of the World Peace Brigade and no plans had been made to pass on the responsibility for initiating new projects to any particular set of persons. However, the tradition of the World Peace Brigade was still very much alive in the memories of those who knew about the work and in plans of others who thought that civilian groups might be formed to act along the lines of the United Nations Forces, but without weapons. Thus it happened that in 1971, discussions were held in India by members of the Shanti Sena (Gandhian Peace Brigade) and in the United States by the staff of the International Peace Academy concerning the possibility of placing "International Peace Contingents" in troubled areas of the world.

After proposing the general idea of Peace Contingents to delegations at the United Nations, the staff of the International Peace Academy suggested to Charles Walker and me, who were then at the Center for Nonviolent Conflict Resolution at Haverford College in the United States, that Cyprus might be a good place to initiate such a project. General Indarjit Rikhye, chairman of the International Peace Academy, had had extensive experience with the United Nations Forces. Brigadier Michael Harbottle, a member of the Peace Academy staff, had been a chief of staff for the United Nations Forces on Cyprus. Both men felt that it would be timely to have a third-party civilian group working alongside of the United Nations Forces. Although a proposal for "Volunteers for Peace: Cyprus Mission" was prepared, it was obvious that more details of the current situation on Cyprus were needed as well as a more detailed indication of the activities of the Cyprus Mission. As a result, a visit of a first team was planned for August 1972.

The First Team

August 1972. A team of five persons visited Cyprus during the first two weeks of August. (The teams were composed of persons with experience in nonviolent action and persons with technical skills. Volunteers were recruited from the United States, United Kingdom, India, and South Africa). Interviews were held with representatives of the United Nations, and Greek and Turkish officials. Mr. Osorio-Tafal, United Nations Representative in Cyprus, suggested that we work on psychological problems that divide people rather than on problems requiring only technical assistance. In particular he suggested that the resettlement of Turkish displaced persons who had left their homes at the "time of troubles" in 1963 was a humanitarian problem that might provide a focus for the work. Officials on the Greek side were already committed to the principal of resettlement and had rebuilt houses in some villages. On the Turkish side officials recalled warmly the work of a group of British volunteers who had rebuilt some houses in a village several years before. However, at this time no progress had been made toward resettlement for some years and persons on the Greek and Turkish sides gave different reasons as to why the Turkish villagers had not returned.

November 1972. As a result of the August visit to Cyprus, a proposal was prepared for the American Friends Service Committee asking for funds and support. However Cyprus did not appear on their list of priorities, and the project was left without any immediate prospect of funding or other support. Also it appeared that it might be difficult to secure support from any funding organization without more formal written indications that officials on the Greek and Turkish sides approved of the project.

March 1973. During a brief visit to Cyprus, I drew up a one-page proposal addressed to the Government of Cyprus concerning the formation of a working party to deal with the problem of the resettlement of displaced Turkish persons in Cypriot villages. The working party would consist of three Greeks, two Turks, and four persons from the international peace movement.

The proposal was endorsed on the same day by a letter from Mr. Rauf Denktash, Vice-President of the Republic of Cyprus, on the Turkish side and by a letter two weeks later from Mr. C. Veniamin, Director-General of the Ministry of Foreign Affairs, on the Greek side. On the basis of the proposal and the endorsements, the Executive Committee of the Lilly Endowment made a grant of $25,000 and the project was under way.

The Second Team

July 1973. A second team of five persons worked on Cyprus. Initially they gathered more detailed information about conditions on Cyprus and the history of the resettlement problem. Reports were written giving the position of the Greek side, the Turkish side, and the United Nations. Throughout the month, team members met with representatives of each side separately as the two sides had not yet agreed to meet face-to-face to discuss the resettlement process. These discussions led to a memorandum giving our understanding of the "next steps toward the resettlement of displaced persons." This proposal was endorsed by both sides.

August 1973. A second grant of $25,000 was received from the Lilly Endowment for the continuation of the project on a larger scale than the remaining funds would allow.

September 1973. I visited India to recruit members of the Shanti Sena for the project.

The Third Team

November 1973 - January 1974. The third and largest team of 18 volunteers arrived to work on Cyprus. This was the period of the most extensive work on the project. There were teams of three or four volunteers living in each of the villages of Dhiorios, Peristerona, Nisou, and Pano Lefkara. Each team collected information related to resettlement from villages in its area and tried to find ways to increase the involvement of the villagers in the resettlement process. Some members helped with negotiations between the Ministry of Foreign Affairs, on the Greek side, and the Turkish Cypriot Leadership.

December 1973. A front-page story in the *Cyprus Mail* about "further aid to displaced Turks" announced the fact that the Government of Cyprus would repair houses of Turkish Cypriots who had left their homes ten years before during the "time of troubles." The next day, the paper quoted Mr. Osorio-Tafal, the United Nations special representative on Cyprus, as saying that this step by the Government "would contribute to more understanding and would create better conditions for furtherance of a solution" to the Cyprus problem. In press releases, both the Greek and Turkish sides noted the contribution of the Cyprus Resettlement Project in helping to facilitate the process of resettlement.

January 1974. After many consultations on both sides of the Green Line, officials from the Greek and Turkish sides met face-to-face with members of the CRP and a representative of the United Nations to discuss the next steps in the resettlement process. There is no written statement describing the purpose of the meeting because we were unable to find a wording for a statement that was acceptable to both sides.

The Fourth Team

April 1974. In mid-April a team of four persons arrived to review the progress towards resettlement and to decide whether or not any further service by the project seemed desirable. They found that a new political development had brought the Inter-Communal Talks to a halt and that the Government had not yet voted the money to begin the reconstruction in the four villages. However, it appeared that the political situation might be "clarified" by the end of May, allowing the work to proceed.

May 1974. As an interim project, to assure some movement towards resettlement and as a sign of the goodwill of the citizens on both sides, the team proposed that a four-week work camp be held in one of the villages, beginning the second week of July. As a final phase of the Cyprus Resettlement Project the team also proposed that after the Greek side had completed building the first set of houses, four volunteers would return to Cyprus for six months. They would live in one or two of the villages and be concerned with all of the villages to which Turkish families were returning. Where necessary, the volunteers would act as third parties on any issues arising from the resettlement and help with plans for the continuation of the resettlement process. The Greek side approved both the plans for the work camp and for the final phase of the project on May 17, 1974.

A third request was made to the Lilly Endowment for funds to support the final six months of the project. This request was never acted upon because the need for funds fell away with the arrival of the Turkish army on July 20.

June-July 1974. Three members of the fourth team had left the island by the end of the first week of May, leaving Ellen Wilkinson to organize the work camp. In June, Dan Sipe arrived to assist her. With the help of business and social groups, funds were raised for the work camp so that building materials could be purchased. The Cyprus government and the CRP also contributed to the building costs. Some materials and supplies were donated. The plan was to rebuild six Turkish houses in one village with the help of about 40 Greek and Turkish students.

The work camp had been underway for one week when there was a coup that replaced the Greek government. Although most of the students left the village, a few stayed behind to continue the work until the Turkish army invaded Cyprus on the 20th of July. Ellen Wilkinson stayed on in the village for about a week until the older Turks had been released from the village mosque where they had been imprisoned. She was then evacuated to London on a British Air Force plane.

Termination of Mission

March 1975. In response to a letter about the possibility of further work on Cyprus, Denktash, now President of the Turkish Federated State of Cyprus, indicated that there was no further need to continue the Cyprus Resettlement Project because the whole situation had changed. There were similar indications from the Greek side.

April 1975. At the end of a one-week visit to Cyprus, I issued a "Termination of Mission Report" after interviewing persons on each side to see if there was a possibility of further work involving resettlement. By this time, Turkish villagers from the south of the island had moved to the northern section controlled by the Turks and there were some 200,000 displaced Greek persons who had moved south. Various international agencies were providing communication between the two sides. Thus the need for the CRP as it was originally formulated had fallen away and no new project could be found that was not already covered by existing agencies.

An Example of Negotiation[2]

One of the small problems we solved on Cyprus that can be used as an example of the consensus method concerned the issue of "trouble makers." When we began our work, we noted that both the Greek and Turkish sides agreed "in principle" that Turkish villagers should be resettled in their villages. However, the United Nations representative had tried to encourage some actual progress towards the reconstruction of houses for many years without success before the initiative for the work was turned over to us. Various problems had to be solved before the building could begin. One problem for the Greek side was that there were said to be "trouble makers" among the Turks who would agitate in the villages when Turks were being moved back in and would make trouble for the Greek officials. After hearing a statement of the problem on the Greek side, we went over to the Turkish side of Nicosia, through the armed checkpoint, to suggest to the Turks a possible solution. "How would it be," we asked, "if the Turkish trouble makers were not allowed to return to the villages?" "No," said the Turks, "we cannot have any of our people branded as trouble makers." We went back to the Greek side to try again and to find out more about "trouble makers." We were told that the trouble makers were only a problem when the villagers were first moving back; after most people had returned to a village, the trouble makers would have little influence.

By this time, we had surveyed the former Turkish villages that were now deserted and the empty Turkish quarters in formerly mixed villages where Greeks were still living; we knew how many houses had been completely or partially destroyed. We also had estimates of the cost of repair and knew that the Greek side would have difficulty finding the funds necessary for a complete rehabilitation of the Turkish quarters. In fact, both sides had agreed that it would be enough to start in a few villages. So we suggested to the Greeks that instead of rebuilding a smaller number of villages completely, they begin by building half of the houses in a larger number of villages. In this way, once the Greeks were given a complete list of the Turkish villagers who wished to return, the Greeks could designate the families to move in first without having to identify a small set of families whose members were likely to cause trouble. The Greek side thought this might work. So we tried it out on the Turkish side. Yes, they would agree. So we had a solution. No one on the Turkish side need be branded as a trouble maker and no one on the Greek side need actually identify the trouble makers who had been presented as a factor preventing the return of the Turks for so many years.

Some Applications of Functional Analysis[3]

In Cyprus, on some occasions I used functional analysis quite consciously to diagnose a problem faced by the group of volunteers either within a group or in relationship to Cypriot society. However most problems were solved on a day-to-day and indeed hour-to-hour basis without explicit reference to any theory. As actors in the situation, we tried to make our best judgements at the time, all things being considered. An observer of our group would have been able to note more examples as the action unfolded. Looking back over our activity, we can identify situations to which we can apply the three major hypotheses: that the content of social interaction can be divided into four functional categories, that groups develop through a sequence of phases, and that the power of factors influencing decisions follows the cybernetic hierarchy of control.

First we can use the AGIL categories to sort out the values held by the members of our team. As third parties we were not "value free." We would not have endorsed social change in any direction by any means. The value on which we placed the greatest stress was the use of *nonviolent* methods of conflict resolution. Our other basic values were perhaps more evident in our actions than in our proclamations, because we had not come to Cyprus to bring about a particular kind of society, but rather to help the Greeks and Turks reach common goals. Still one could identify in each of the four functional areas values that were shared by most of the members of the teams. We should note that there was variation, even on the issue of nonviolence. However, we expect a group of this kind continually to examine the basic values of its members as it attempts to find solutions to social problems in the light of these shared values. Examples of the ideas about the ideal society that were represented in our approach are:

(A) Economic: There should be an equal distribution of resources.
(G) Political: The society should provide for maximum autonomy and self control.
(I) Legal/social class: The society should minimize social distinctions and maximize integration and belonging.
(L) Religious: There should be a supreme value placed on human life, minimizing religious differences (we are all human beings).

The phases in group development are most easily seen in the development of the whole project. First, even in developing the idea of the project there were four phases that could be considered as subphases of "L," or defining the basic meaning. The original idea for peace contingents came from the Gandhians and the Peace Academy (L_1). To test the idea for Cyprus we needed to raise seed money to finance the first visit (L_a). With the seed money, we were able to assemble a team and decide on our roles (L_i). Then on Cyprus, we were able to select a particular focus for the work (L_g). Once the Greeks and Turks had agreed on our proposal, we again had to raise money (A) and assemble and train a team (I) to act as third parties in reaching the first agreement (G). This cycle was repeated in the development of the work-camp idea. Termination brought the final phase of "L" when we once again had to sort out "the meaning of all this" for volunteers, for Cyprus, and for the future of transnational efforts at conflict resolution.

Our conscious use of the cybernetic hierarchy of control in making decisions is evident within the teams, where we use consensus rather than voting. Our emphasis on values rather than on economic gain is also evident in our approach to the Greek and Turkish sides. We help them find "non-zero-sum" solutions that are based on humanitarian motives rather than those that are primarily concerned with redistribution of resources or of political power. Recall that Mr. Osorio-Tafal of the United Nations had suggested that we help with the return of displaced persons because it could be seen as a "humanitarian problem." Thus our task was made easier than if we had been asked to help with the whole "Cyprus problem," which requires a political solution.

We believe that the same nonviolent third-party process can be used with problems that are basically political. The Gandhians have experience in India in developing the "Gramdan" or village government movement for formerly landless people (the "untouchables") who now own land communally and manage their own village affairs for the first time in history. In 1974, some Gandhians, including Narayan Desai, the head of Shanti Sena, and other people who had served with the Cyprus project were asked to take over as an interim government in some states in India. Members of the state governments had resigned in the face of charges of corruption and the Gandhians made the "political" decisions until new governments could be formed.

From time to time, members of the Greek or Turkish sides made remarks that indicated they understood and appreciated our approach. After we had negotiated the agreement to hold a work camp, a representative of the Ministry of Foreign Affairs told us that the Government found it easy to approve of the project because, after all, we were doing it "for Cyprus."

On Cyprus, with all of the resources of the United Nations available, one might have thought that a small group could add little. Yet for all the 3,000 men in the United Nations force, only seven were involved in work with communities and only two in political negotiations.

Levels of Creativity in Decisions

Throughout the Cyprus Project, we can find examples of decisions at different levels of creativity. For example, the decision to have the Greek and Turkish sides meet at the conference table without a formal statement of purpose, and the decision to begin building houses in two phases so that trouble makers need not be identified, are both at the lowest level of creativity. Each side maintains the position they had on the issues but the critical subjects are simply avoided. An example of the next highest level, that involving skill, would be the selection of the team members for the various third-party teams. Rather than provide training—for people already on Cyprus—in the nonviolent approach and the use of consensus as well as various social science skills, teams were composed of persons who already had the desired backgrounds. The composition of the teams also included an element of the next highest level, that of combinations, as it was assumed that this particular combination of persons—old and young, male and female, a variety of backgrounds relevant to nonviolence and to resettlement—would be the most effective.

Using a work camp involving Greek and Turkish youths to demonstrate the possibility of cooperation in rebuilding houses for Turkish villagers is an example of creativity at the extension of theory level (innovative). The idea of a work camp was not new and had been used by many groups, including Quakers, to give youths from different cultural backgrounds the experience of working together on some community project. However, on previous occasions, the work camp was not seen as a model for a national effort of a similar kind. Even where the youth project was connected to a national goal, as in the massive campaign of "Youth Against Famine" in India led by Narayan Desai (1972: 51-54), the main focus was on the contribution of youth to the society. In the Cyprus case, the work camp constituted a variation on the usual theme, because the camp provided a channel for citizen initiative on a long-standing problem while waiting for the official government project to begin.

Although a decision at any of the lower levels of creativity alters the previous set of conditions and thus represents a new definition of the situation at that level, I am not aware that any of our work on Cyprus provided anyone with an entirely new view of the problems of resettlement. Thus there are no examples of creativity at the highest level.

Summary

Conflict resolution requires creativity to invent a solution for the conflict. Simply having people who can get on together to discuss the issue and who have good decision procedures is not enough.

The Cyprus Resettlement Project, which was active from 1972 through 1974, consisted of ad hoc groups of persons working parallel to the United Nations Forces on Cyprus. As third parties, they helped the Greek and Turkish sides initiate a program for the resettlement of displaced Turkish persons who had left their homes in the villages during the "time of troubles" in 1963. The four CRP teams that visited the island over the two-year period were composed of volunteers from India, England, U.S.A., and South Africa, who had experience with or a commitment to the nonviolent solution of problems. They worked in the tradition of the World Peace Brigade and the Indian Shanti Sena (Peace Brigade).

Team members helped collect information about the condition of houses in the villages and the families who wished to return. They also arranged a face-to-face meeting of representatives of the Greek and Turkish sides to discuss the program and organized a workcamp of Greek and Turkish youth to begin to rebuild Turkish houses. The coup and the invasion of the mainland Turkish army in July 1974 brought all activity to a halt.

The application of the AGIL functional categories to CRP activities is used to illustrate the values held by team members in the four functional areas. The group was seen to develop through the functional areas in the L-A-I-G sequence with a Terminal L stage.

Throughout the project, decisions were made that represented levels of creativity from the lowest—that of avoiding a problem—to the use of skill, combination, and the extension of an idea. However no decision appeared to give an entirely new definition of the situation.

Notes

1. Hare and Wilkinson (1977) give some details of the project and Hare (1984) provides the most complete report and is the source of the descriptive material in this chapter.

2. From A. P. Hare, "Third party conflict resolution: Cyprus pre 1974 and South Africa post 1976." Paper presented at the International Workshop on Conflict Resolution held at the Jewish-Arab Center, Institute of Middle East Studies, University of Haifa, Israel, June 1978.

3. The section on functional analysis of some aspects of the Cyprus project is reprinted from Hare (1977: 278-280).

Chapter 5

Ethnic Groups in Namibia and South Africa

We return to Southern Africa for three cases of conflict resolution where different ethnic groups were involved in creating new forms of social organization. In the first case, representatives of various "population groups" met in the Turnhalle in Windhoek, Namibia (South West Africa) to draft a constitution using consensus as a decision method. In the second case, "Coloured" residents of Cape Town, South Africa, staged a mass nonviolent protest on a street that had been used only the week before as the scene of a violent and deadly attack by police on a stone-throwing crowd. In the third case, workers from the Ford Motor Company plant in Port Elizabeth, South Africa, were assisted in resolving a conflict with management by the American Consul-General acting as a third party.[1]

Turnhalle Conference, Namibia

In 1975 in Namibia, representatives of all population groups were called together at the Turnhalle in Windhoek to develop a constitution for an area that appeared to be on the verge of independence. Rather than take decisions by majority vote, they decided to use the method of consensus. Although Dirk Mudge, one of the organizers of the conference, and the other delegates had made no conscious study of consensus, their use of method is similar in its basic approach to that developed by the Society of Friends (Quakers) over a period of 300 years (Hare, 1982: 146-154, 163-174), and to the way in which the consensus method is usually described in the social psychological literature on group decision making (Scheff, 1967; Dodd and Christopher, 1969; Hare, 1976: 344-345). One of the most complete sets of rules for laboratory groups was developed by Hall and Watson (1970) and adapted by Nemiroff and King (1975). However, in common with most studies of consensus, the focus was on the consequences of the decision method rather than on the process.

The delegations that arrived for the Conference differed markedly in size and in the ways in which they were constituted. Some of the delegates were traditional Chiefs, some elected leaders, some appointed leaders, and some chosen because their skills or backgrounds were especially relevant. Although the composition and representativeness of the various delegations was a controversial issue, the South West Africa Peoples Organization (SWAPO) was not included, a detailed description of the delegations is not necessary for the present analysis, as the decision process used in the Constitutional Conference was not influenced in any obvious way by the composition of the delegations. The total number of delegates for each population group, listed in alphabetical order (as they would appear in Afrikaans) was as follows:

Baster	12
White (Blankes)	3
Bushman	2
Caprivi	8
Damara	31
Herero	44
Kavango	8
Coloured (Kleurling)	11
Nama	29
Ovambo	15
Tswana	6

During the recruiting phase, Mr. Mudge, one of the organizers, suggested that the Conference should make decisions by discussing issues until everyone agreed, without voting.

Although Mr. Mudge was clear about the advantages of having a full discussion of the issue before reaching a decision that would satisfy all parties, he did not have a detailed conception of the procedures to be followed under a "consensus" method. When asked how he explained the use of consensus to the prospective delegates during the recruiting phase, he responded, "I'm afraid you will be disappointed now. I never thought about it that way. The only thing I told them was that we cannot vote. If we do vote, the minority groups will have no chance at all. We have Ovambos, for instance, representing 50 per cent of the population. The Whites are the second largest group. But we also have the Coloureds and the Basters, and the Tswanas with only 5,000 persons. I tried to explain to them that if we would vote the minority groups would have no say at all. So we decided that the only way it can be done, without in any way dominating or forcing any minority group, will be to reach consensus. This will be a protection for the smaller groups. But I never made a study of this. Really, sir, I feel you must be disappointed. It happened by coincidence, I would say."

Even though consensus was urged as the decision method for the meetings of the Constitutional Conference, it was left free for each delegation to decide which method of decision making they would use to formulate their internal policy. Some delegations used majority vote, whereas others used a discussion method that is closer to the traditional African "indaba."[2]

Throughout the whole process, many decisions needed to be made concerning the economic, political and social organization of the new independent country. Although recordings were made of the work of the committees, these records were not made public because it was an important feature of the conference that the delegates be free to consider, and reject or accept, proposals without being bound by public statements on the discussions that might appear in the press. In 1977, when the Turnhalle conference was disbanded and reorganized as a political party, the government impounded all of the files. Thus, for the present analysis, we have two examples of decisions as recalled by Dr. Africa, chairman of the Baster Delegation, that were made during the drafting of the "Declaration of Intent." Dr. Africa recalled some of the general features of the discussion around some of the early issues, as examples of "give and take" as follows (Hare and von Broembsen, 1979: 17ff.):

> The issues were whether to call South West Africa by its usual name or to refer to it as "Namibia" and how much emphasis to place on ethnic differences in the Declaration of Intent. Some delegates preferred the name Namibia and did not even want to mention South West Africa. Some delegates felt that ethnic differences were being emphasised too much. The final version of the declaration represents a middle way.

Neither the delegates who wanted Namibia nor the ones who wanted to emphasize the real ethnic differences carried the decision. South West Africa is referred to as a geographical entity and population groups are mentioned rather than ethnic groups.

A second example of "give and take" was the discussion of petty apartheid in hotels. Previously any hotels who wanted to open their doors for persons of any color had to apply for a permit. One group of delegates felt that there should be certain requirements and that patrons must adhere to a certain standard. Others felt that this was not important and they did not even want the right to admission reserved. In this case agreement was reached on a proposal that hotel owners would not need to apply for permission, but could reserve the right of admission so that the hotel manager could bar patrons who did not meet an acceptable standard of dress and behavior.

Images of Decisions at the Turnhalle

Field diagrams representing two of the decisions described by Dr. Africa are given in Figure 5.1. The top diagram shows the images of "South West Africa as a State" and "Namibia" as circles with solid outlines. The image of South West Africa as a state is strong (upward), positive, serious, and conforming to the traditional use of European names. In contrast, the image presented by the term "Namibia" is also strong (upward), and serious, but somewhat hostile (negative) and rebellious (anticonforming), keeping with the tendency to use African-based terms for names of new black states. Thus the images appear in opposite quadrants of the field diagram, one as UPSC whereas the other is UNSA. A compromise is found along the line connecting the midpoint of the two image circles and midway between them. The concept of South West Africa as a geographical entity is not as strong (upward) as the other two concepts—serious, and fairly neutral with regard to the positive-negative and conforming-anticonforming dimensions (dashed circle).

The lower field diagram shows a similar effect for the decision concerning permits for hotels. In this case, the image presented by the idea of reserving the right of admission to hotels is UNSC, whereas the image of hotels that are open to all is UPEA. The compromise solution is to combine the two ideas, an example of creativity at Level 3 (combinations). The new rule does not require a permit but still leaves it open for hotel owners to reserve the right of admission if they wish to. This solution can be seen on the field diagram as a large dashed circle that intercepts both previous positions. It is represented

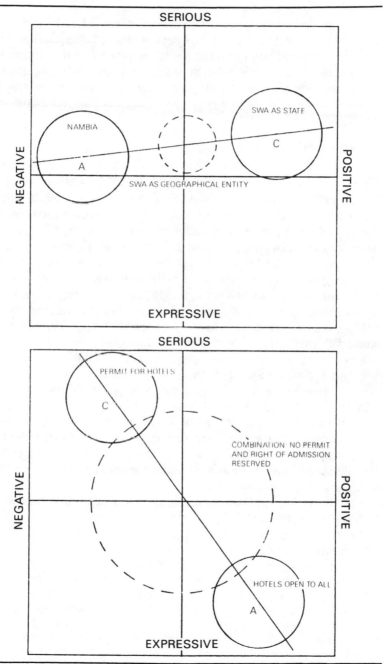

Figure 5.1   Field Diagrams of Images of Decision at Turnhalle Conference

as a large circle (upward) because it allows for more involvement and creativity by the individual hotel owners. Because some hotel owners may wish to take advantage of the negative, serious, and conforming, aspects of the rule, whereas others use the permission to be expressive, and anticonforming, the resulting position of the concept would be neutral on both positive-negative and forward-backward dimensions.

Cape Town, South Africa

The events before and during a funeral at Elsies River in Cape Town in 1980—in the midst of the school boycott—are used to illustrate another aspect of dramaturgical analysis. Here we focus on the "stage" and its importance in understanding an event. We see that without any formal arrangement on the part of those present, including police, protestors, and onlookers, some agreement occurs about the location of the "stage" on which the main action takes place. Anyone who is "offstage" may be either assumed to be part of the audience (if they are facing the stage) or some additional actors preparing to come on the scene (if they are backstage). Often with large crowds or in cramped quarters, it may be difficult to distinguish the active theme carriers on stage from the more passive audience. This was the case at Sharpeville, where the use of high velocity bullets by the police made the distinction between actors and audience less relevant.

In Cape Town in 1980, we will consider the effect of staging on two events, the first when the police killed two youths who were part of a stone-throwing street crowd, and the second when a funeral for the youths was held several days later. In the first instance, the police controlled the staging as directors, and in the second, members of the community played a major part.

As I was involved in some of the activity, my account is written in the first person (Hare, 1983b: 91-94):

In the later part of May some scholars had shifted the focus from demonstrations at school to attempts to disrupt major shopping centers. In some areas buses and cars were stoned and transportation was disrupted. One of the areas where the reactions of crowds and police was most violent was Elsies River, the poorest residential section of the Coloured community. On Wednesday, May 28, police wearing civilian clothes set a trap for persons who were throwing stones by driving up and down on a major thoroughfare in an unmarked "kombie." When stones were eventually thrown at the vehicle, policemen jumped up from where they had been hidden in the back and opened fire on the crowd, killing two youths, one a 15-year-old scholar. This incident and follow-up stories provided front-page headlines for the next few days. The "trouble areas" were reported as calm, but tense. Funerals were scheduled for the following Monday.

A week or so before the shooting incident the representatives of UTASA (Union of Teachers' Association of South Africa) had called a meeting to which church leaders and other community leaders had been invited to provide a broader base for discussion and action concerning the schools' boycott. A steering committee under Bishop Naidoo of the Catholic Church had been appointed to plan further meetings of the group and to work out guidelines for action. I was asked to join the committee as a consultant. On Wednesday, May 28, the first meeting of the steering committee was interrupted with news of the deaths in Elsies River. A meeting was hastily called for that Friday to discuss this event and the other issues that faced the community. Since it had often happened that funerals of members of the black community had been the occasions for funeral orations that had a political flavour, and since police had often killed or injured people in their attempt to disperse the crowd at graveside, we wanted to avoid a replication of the pattern at the funeral the following week.

At the end of the Friday meeting I made a short list of the persons who needed to be contacted to assure that the funeral would be a peaceful event and that police would be kept in the background. With the help of a few persons at the meeting the riot police were asked to remain in the background. The local traffic police were advised that we would have "marshals" to control the crowd. The minister at the church where the funeral services was to be held and the family of the scholar were notified of our plans and asked if there was anything we could do to help them. In addition, a minister who had already been asked to speak at graveside agreed to speak to the crowd to help keep order should the police attack at that point in the service. It was also important that members of the "Committee of 81" (student representatives of the Coloured high schools who were acting as spokesmen for the protesting students) give their approval to the arrangement. However, as they were being sought after by the police we could not expect them to attend any sort of organizational meeting, so they were notified through third parties. Through this same network arrangements were made to have students from the Coloured Teachers College act as marshals. They wore their school blazers and used loud hailers. I had at first thought that no one from the Coloured community might wish to take the highly visible 'marshal' role and had considered asking white women from the Black Sash and the Women's Movement for Peace to play this role. However, once we knew that marshals could be obtained from the Coloured community, this proved to be a much better solution. As a final precaution I arranged to have two ambulances on hand from the "Voluntary Service" (a group organized as an example of voluntary national service that might be performed by conscientious objectors). I drove one of the ambulances.

The *Cape Times* (Tuesday, June 3) carried the following account of the funeral:

ELSIES RIVER MOURNS HALT RD DEATHS
by YAZEED FAKIER

Elsies River mourned yesterday as pupils, churchmen and parents turned up to attend the joint funeral service of 15-year-old Bernard Fortuin and William Lubbe, 20, who were shot dead after police opened fire on crowds of stone-throwers in Halt Road last Wednesday.

The massive funeral service, conducted at the St. Nicholas Anglican Church, Halt Road, Elsies River, was watched by newsmen including representatives of the BBC, United Press International, Associated Press and Visnews.

From about 12 p.m., buses with loads of school children started trickling into Elsies River and by the time the service started at 2.10 p.m. about 12 000 people were present.

Traffic police were out in force at the scene as traffic was brought to a standstill along Halt Road. Student "marshals" from Hewat Training College stood at strategic points and did well in controlling the crowd.

Pupils, black and Coloured, from almost all the schools in the Peninsula attended the service.

Dr. Allan Boesak, University of the Western Cape student chaplain, told the mass gathering: "I believe the deaths of Bernard and William were totally unnecessary. And if we had had a place to live as human beings, where we could live freely with one another, to serve one another and where the love of God was allowed to reign freely in our hearts, this would not have happened."

The principal of Elnor Primary School said the suffering of Bernard's family was shared by the people of South Africa and all over the world.

He said those pupils who had died in the struggle, died so that their brothers and sisters might live for a better tomorrow.

There were no incidents and no injuries. Our ambulances took part in the funeral procession, one at midpoint and the other bringing up the

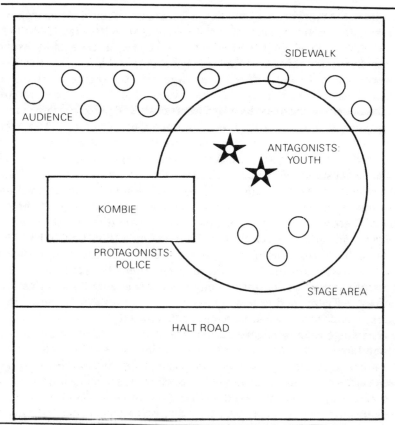

Figure 5.2   Scene of Shooting at Halt Road

rear. Our services were used only by two women, each of whom required an aspirin tablet for a headache.

Staging Events in Cape Town

Figure 5.2 represents the actors and audience on the scene at Halt Road when the police shot the two youths. Prior to this scene the police had been driving up and down Halt Road, with only the driver in plain clothes visible to the crowd, waiting for someone to throw stones at them. There is a similarity in their action and that of the actors who staged "morality plays" in England many years ago. The actors in the morality play would go from town to town with a wagon, looking for an appropriate audience. When an audience assembled, the actors would mount the bed of the wagon as a stage and present their drama in which they hoped to bring a moral message to the crowd. The police at Elsies River were also the theme carriers, or protagonists, for a theme of "law and order" that they hoped to impart to the people of the area. In order to make their drama most effective they needed someone to act as an antagonist, in this case to throw stones. So up and down the street they went until some antagonist was induced to play his or her part. At this point, the police actors emerged from "backstage" in the unmarked kombi and a small section of the street and sidewalk became the stage or action area. Anyone within the action area was assumed to be "onstage" and was subject to being shot. There was little time for the police to try to distinguish between actors and audience. Once the 15-year-old schoolboy fell to the ground, bleeding, some members of the audience tried to come forward to give first aid, but the police ordered them to leave the stage, possibly so that the moral message in the scene could have its full impact. After the bodies had been removed, the street became again a background for more ordinary everyday activity.

The stage area in Figure 5.3, on the day of the funeral, covers a much larger space than that of the shooting. The "play" to be performed will have at least three main acts: first at the church during the funeral service, then during the procession of several kilometers to the cemetery, and finally at graveside. During each act, a large crowd of participants and spectators is expected to be present. Although some individual actors will be present, the main part of the activity will be carried out by groups: family groups, groups of scholars, and groups of police. If the theme of violence and counter-violence is to be avoided, then the members of the community with the cooperation of the police must ensure that the group that symbolizes potential violence—such as the riot police and gangs of "skollies"—are kept away from the scene and nonviolent "marshals" and well-disciplined groups of scholars in school uniforms are allowed to set the tone. Fortunately there was cooperation on all sides for the period of the action, although the police did arrest the woman who acted as "chief marshal" the next day. Thus the event demonstrates the importance of staging—that is, the same street that serves as a backdrop for a tragedy of violent action on one day can be used to demonstrate the possibilities for nonviolent action on the next.

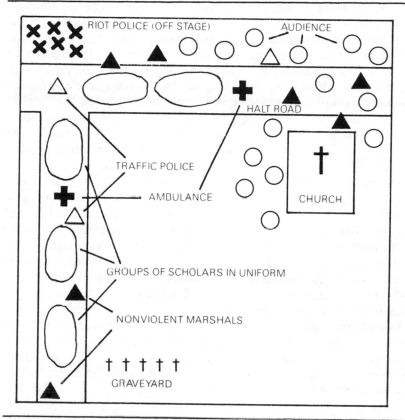

RIOT POLICE (OFF STAGE)

AUDIENCE

HALT ROAD

TRAFFIC POLICE

AMBULANCE

CHURCH

GROUPS OF SCHOLARS IN UNIFORM

NONVIOLENT MARSHALS

GRAVEYARD

Figure 5.3   Scene of Funeral at Elsies River

Ford Motor Company Strike, South Africa

In 1979, a strike occurred at the Ford Motor Company plant in Port Elizabeth, South Africa (Hare, 1983b: 124-129). At this time, part of the job of Alan W. Lukens as U.S. Consul-General in Cape Town was to keep in touch with Port Elizabeth and more specifically the American companies there. After the publication of the "Sullivan Principles" as guidelines for American companies in South Africa, he wished to know how they were being followed. The best way to get the feeling of the labor scene was to get to know workers in the American companies as well as other people in the communities from which the workers are drawn. So he had come to know the Port Elizabeth Black Civic Organization (PEBCO), a community action group that had started out by trying to obtain a better deal on rents and other modest reforms. But it happened that most of the PEBCO leaders also worked for the Ford Motor Company. When the strike took place, Ford made the unfortunate decision to throw out Thozamile Botha, who was head of PEBCO, because they thought that he was spending too much time on PEBCO activities. There had been enough in the local papers about the activities of PEBCO and Thozamile Botha so that anyone in middle-level and top management in Port Elizabeth should have known who he was. However, when the other workers went on strike on his behalf, Ford management was surprised.

The workers were sitting around on the company grounds discussing the situation when the police arrived and surrounded them. The workers were convinced that the police were called by the company, although the company always denied it. The workers were threatened and told to go home if they were not going back to work.

News of this incident got back to the Ford headquarters in Detroit where top management did know who Thozamile was. A message was sent to Port Elizabeth advising the local South African managers not to fire Botha, but local management did not know how to turn the situation around. It was still hard for management to believe that workers would go on strike in sympathy with one of their fellow workers. They assumed that workers would work no matter what happened to one of their fellows. However, management found out that they could not run the plant without the workers who went on strike. First, there was such solidarity in the black community that others would not offer themselves up for jobs, although management tried hard to find workers in the Coloured community. Second, there were no other skilled workers available. These people were not floor sweepers, they were essential to the manufacture of Fords. It took about a month for management to realize this. In the meantime they kept advertising in the papers and tried to find "scab" labor, but they were not able to find enough.

The strike went on. Detroit advised Port Elizabeth management not to fire the workers. The plant closed down a week early for Christmas so that the situation could cool. Part of the background for Detroit's interest in the case included the fact that a new plant was just then being set up in Nigeria. It would have made things more difficult in Nigeria if it were to become known that there were labor-management problems in South Africa. On the other hand, the local management faced informal pressure from other businessmen who felt that they were giving in to labor's demands.

When Mr. Lukens arrived at the end of the first week of January, the company manager was in Detroit, and Mr. Fred Ferreira, the Industrial Relations Manager of the plant, was in charge. By this time, the company realized that they needed the workers back because they could not make Fords without them. From his conversation with some of the workers, Mr. Lukens knew that they really wanted to go back. The union had no money. The churches had helped some, but by now the workers were really suffering. They had not been paid since sometime in November and had missed their Christmas bonuses. Although Mr. Ferreira would have preferred to have the workers meet in his office, Mr. Lukens suggested that they meet in a hotel room as a netural place. Following this suggestion, Ford took a suite in the Elizabeth Hotel.

Mr. Lukens agreed to ask the workers to come, provided he could tell them that Ford management was serious about talking and that the company was considering taking the workers back. The workers would need to know that they were not just going to be started again at the bottom. Because some of the men had been working in the plant for ten to 15 years, they could not just be taken back as floor-sweepers. They would all have to be taken back in the same positions at the same rates of pay. They should have their pensions and medical rights. Mr. Ferreira said that the company would consider these points. Mr. Lukens responded that he would not even ask the workers to meet if the company could not agree to these basic points. When Port Elizabeth management called Detroit, they were advised to go ahead and begin negotiations along the lines that had been discussed.

At first Mr. Ferreira was reluctant to tell the workers what the company was prepared to do, but he then agreed that there was no need to spend a whole day discussing something that the company was prepared to agree to from the start. However, the question of the Christmas bonus was left open for further discussion.

Mr. Lukens then held a meeting with Thozamile Botha and some of the other leaders of the workers in his hotel room at the Holiday Inn. They agreed to meet with Ford.

The actual negotiations were held in the suite in the Elizabeth Hotel. The Ford Company had asked that Johny Mke, head of the company union, be present at the talks. He had already discredited himself in the eyes of the workers by appearing to side with management in telling the men to go back to work. However, Botha and the

PEBCO representatives, along with George Manase, the general secretary of the union, had agreed that Mke could come. There was a sign in the lobby of the hotel to the effect that a "Ford Labor Conference" was being held on the fifth floor. Mr. Lukens arrived a little early to find that Mr. Ferreira and his assistant Mr. Dirk Pieterse were the only ones present. There were two rooms, one with a large green cloth-covered table, and the other totally empty. As no arrangements had been made to meet the delegation of workers, Mr. Lukens went down to the lobby and found Botha and the PEBCO men huddled in the parking lot wondering what to do. They all went up to the conference room where the others were still awaiting the union men. George Manase had arrived, but no arrangement had been made to give Mr. Mke time off from work to attend the meeting or for transportation to bring him to the hotel. So the plant was phoned and a company car ordered.

Although Mr. Ferreira wanted to wait until Mr. Mke arrived before beginning discussions, Mr. Lukens suggested they begin with more general issues, leaving the formal part until the union head arrived. After introducing the groups to each other, and noting that there was goodwill on both sides, Mr. Lukens was prepared to leave them to their discussions and made as if to leave. However, from their reaction he could see that he could not beg out at that point. As an opening statement, he said that he understood from the Ford management that they were willing to take the workers back and reinstate them. First the meeting discussed the fringe benefits without disagreement and then came to the Christmas bonus, which was the bone of contention. After some discussion, it was agreed that it was reasonable that the workers only be given a bonus for the months they had actually worked. The next issue was, when would the men go back to work? Ford wanted to screen everyone and in particular did not want to rehire "ringleaders." Of course, some of the "ringleaders" were actually at the meeting. If everyone was to be rehired, Ford asked, what was to be done with the 100 or so persons who had been hired to fill places when the regular workers were on strike? Mr. Lukens noted that the Financial Mail was predicting a boom so that the company might be able to use all the workers. After a long discussion, during which the company explained its difficult financial position, the company agreed to take everyone back with screening.

The meeting then discussed the meaning of the term "screening." Unfortunately the term had an offensive side to it in the minds of the workers. As the workers already knew their way around the plant, they could find their way back to the assembly line and begin work. However, the workers agreed that if screening only meant filling out new forms, they could do this, but they did not want to be screened by the police. So the issue was left at that.

In the middle of the discussion, after the meeting had been going on from about 9:00 a.m. until 12:00 p.m., Mr. Lukens proposed that they stop to have something to eat and drink. So beer and sandwiches were ordered from room service at Ford's expense.

After an agreement had been reached, Mr. Lukens asked what would be done to authenticate the agreement. Noting that the press was outside, it was agreed that the meeting should prepare a communiqué to be given to the press to sum up what had been decided. As they drafted the communiqué, it was apparent that the company only reluctantly had agreed to take everyone back and that the date by which this would be done had not yet been set. The company suggested that they would take everyone back as soon as business conditions warranted it. However, Mr. Lukens indicated that this might be too vague for the workers, and proposed that, as this was the middle of January, allowing time for red tape, workers be taken back by February 1st. Mr. Ferreira said that the company had a problem, as their personnel workers could only screen a few workers a day. In response, Mr. Lukens said that it might be possible for Ford to find some extra people to welcome back the workers. The point concerning the reinstatement of workers at their former positions was again discussed as management asked what was to be done with the substitute workers who had been hired in the meantime. This was a touchy point that led Thozamile Botha to make a political speech, which did not move matters forward. As a compromise, Mr. Lukens suggested the phrase "positions which they had before or positions similar to those, while waiting for those positions to become available."

When the draft of the communiqué was complete, there was a question of who would sign it and what they would call themselves. The Ford managers had no problem signing themselves but said that the company did not recognize the union and did not recognize PEBCO. Because everyone was in the room, and all had agreed to the communiqué, Mr. Lukens suggested that they all just sign their names without any titles. So they did just that.

After the communique was drafted, it was typed by a secretary on the hotel staff and copies were made on the hotel duplicating machine. These copies were then handed out to the group and to the waiting press and the meeting turned into a press conference.

That night, Thozamile Botha had already arranged a meeting at Walmer. He was arrested on his way to the meeting. Although this may not have had anything to do with the meeting in the morning, workers believed that they had won a major victory and then Ford had sabotaged it by calling in the police. Mr. Lukens pointed out to the workers that the police would not have even heard about the agreement until the next day's press so that the plan to arrest Botha must have been made before. However, it is doubtful that the workers were convinced.

Mr. Lukens had to return to Cape Town the next day. Things seemed to be under control at that point. A week later, when Dick Moose, the U.S. Assistant Secretary of Africa, was visiting, Mr. Lukens went back to Port Elizabeth with him and they had a private session with the Ford workers. Aside from the fact that Thozamile was in jail, the workers were happy with the outcome of the meeting. At a private dinner with Ford management, Mr. Lukens and Mr. Moose were told that Ford appreciated the help that had been given. It was clear that both sides had benefited from the agreement and were willing to say so privately, if not publicly.

Workers were taken back, but the process moved slowly. Mr. Lukens was asked again to intervene by the trustees. When he called Ford at Port Elizabeth, he was told that they did not have the manpower in personnel to work any faster so he cautioned the workers to be patient. After about three weeks, Ford had finally taken everyone back except for the nine or ten people who were in the group that had been involved in the negotiations. Ford management said that the problem was that these people could not pass the medical examination. Mr. Lukens impressed management with the fact that these, of all people, would have to be taken back or the whole deal would collapse. Finally, a few days later these last workers were reinstated.

The next crisis came when management refused to discuss the bonus issue that had still not been resolved. It is probable that management felt pressure from industrial colleagues in Port Elizabeth to hold out on the bonus. The issue took about a year to settle. The workers were finally given about three-quarter's of the yearly bonus. Management's line of reasoning was that if a worker quit during the year, he would not be entitled to any bonus. Management was finally able to agree to paying the amount by calling it something else than "last year's bonus."

This was essentially the end of the negotiations concerning the strike. From time to time in the months that followed, Mr. Lukens was called by the workers to help if he could when some of their leaders were arrested and to try to secure the release of Thozamile Botha from prison. There was little he could do. Although Mr. Lukens remained in contact with some of the members of the black community in Port Elizabeth, he was not called to intervene in any other labor-management disputes nor did he think it would have been appropriate as it was only his special relationship to a firm with U.S. connections that provided the entrée on this occasion.

Creativity at Ford Negotiations

For the dramaturgical analysis of the Ford Motor Company strike, the "play" in the form of negotiations leading to a joint press release will be the focus of attention. Because the account of the negotiations was based on an interview with Alan Lukens, it is quite probable that he remembered more of the details of his own contributions. Other than the comments that certain agreements were reached "after some discussion," we have no indication of whether it was Ford management or the workers who eventually found solutions to the problems. Thus we can only assume that there must have been some creativity at Level 3, combinations, or Level 4, extensions of theory, by both workers and management. This underlying level of creativity is indicated in Figure 5.4. It is also quite likely that Mr. Lukens intervened as a third party primarily when the other two could not reach agreement or when the negotiations appeared to be at an impasse for some other reason. Thus the peaks of his creative activity, as shown in Figure 5.4 give us, literally, the high points in the negotiations.

The analysis begins by drawing a time line for the duration of the meeting, marked at one-hour intervals. Although Mr. Lukens tells us that the meeting began at 9 a.m. with a break at 12 noon for lunch, he does not tell us when the meeting ended. In another account of the strike, Maree (1983) records that there were "eight hours of hard bargaining," so we may assume that the negotiations ended about 5 p.m. The time line is next divided into natural time periods when the dominant content of the activity, in terms of the four functional problems, AGIL, remained the same. This gives us seven time periods or acts. Although with a more detailed account of the process, each act could probably be divided into a number of scenes as the specific topic or the people involved in the discussion changed; we have information only about the subperiods within the first act that contained four scenes.

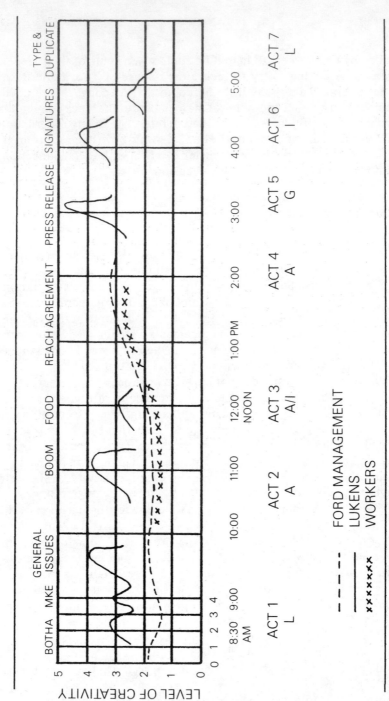

Figure 5.4 Creativity at Ford Negotiations

114

Act 1 begins when Mr. Lukens arrives "a little early" for the conference and ends after his opening statement to the conference. The primary activity is in the L area as it has to do with ensuring that the delegates are all present and defining the initial goals of the conference. There are four scenes. In the first scene, Mr. Lukens arrives and finds that the representatives of Ford management are the only ones present. In scene 2, Mr. Lukens takes the initiative to go to the ground floor to look for the representatives of the black workers. This is indicated in Figure 5.4 as a rise to Level 3 on the graph representing the involvement and creativity of Mr. Lukens. On his return to the conference room, Mr. Lukens finds that no arrangements have been made for the head of the workers' union to attend the meeting. In scene 3, he again takes the initiative to make the necessary arrangements. In the fourth scene, he opens the conference by introducing the groups to each other and suggesting that they begin with general issues until the union representative can arrive. The scene ends and the opening act concludes as Mr. Lukens attempts to step down from his coordinating role. However he senses that he is still needed as the group moves to act 2.

Assuming as we do in this case, and in the case of the negotiations at Camp David described in the next chapter, that the goal of the conference is to produce a document expressing the agreements of the parties in conflict, then the preliminary discussions during which facts are gathered concerning the points of view and requirements of each side constitute activity in the A area. The final goal-attainment work (G) often requires a different definition of roles than those required during the L and A stages, the activity of creating these new roles is in the I area.

In the present case, act 2 begins shortly after 9 a.m. after Mr. Lukens's introduction and ends with the break for lunch at 12 noon. The activity is primarily in the A area. During this act, Mr. Lukens introduces a creative idea by suggesting that a financial boom that had been predicted should make it possible to keep the additional workers on the payroll who had been hired to fill the places of the strikers and also to rehire all of the strikers.

The idea of a lunch break, act 3, is also at the suggestion of Mr. Lukens. It seems that the Ford management had made no provision for lunch. The suggestion to order beer and sandwiches from room service also avoided any embarrassment that might be involved in serving the group containing both blacks and whites. In functional terms, the luncheon provided necessary resources (A) and also probably provided a note of informality in the proceedings (I), although Mr. Lukens does not mention this in his account.

Act 4 continues in the A area until the two sides reach agreement. However no one had suggested the form in which the agreement should be recorded. Presumably sensing the difficulties that would be involved if the Ford management representatives were asked to agree to a formal contract, Mr. Lukens suggested a press release. This was probably his most creative suggestion and is rated as Level 5. As it turned out, no more formal arrangement was ever made and the press release served as the working document that facilitated the ending of the strike and the return of the workers. By drafting the press release, the goal had been achieved, hence the activity is in the G area and makes up act 5.

However the crisis and the need for innovation had not yet passed. The Ford management did not recognize either the union or the community representatives and would not agree to have them sign in their "official" capacities. thus some way needed to be found to redefine the roles of the participants so that the signing could take place and the press release could be given to the press. This adjustment of roles is an activity in the I area and in the typical progression of group development would have preceded the G stage. Once again, Mr. Lukens comes forward with the solution to have everyone sign their names without any titles. Although the signing may have taken only a few minutes, because of the importance of the activity, it has been designated act 6.

Act 7, the notification of the press, provides both a terminal L phase for the negotiating group and a beginning L phase for those who will need to implement the decision. As a final act in his role as the good shepherd, Mr. Lukens arranges to have the press communique typed by a hotel secretary and copied on the hotel duplicating machine.

During the course of the negotiations, none of the innovative ideas presented by Mr. Lukens were momentous in themselves, but they did allow the process to move forward when it might have foundered on some relatively simple issue.

Summary

At the Turnhalle in Windhoek, Namibia in 1975, representatives of various population groups met to draft a constitution for the area that appeared to be on the verge of independence. They used consensus as a decision rule, although they had no formal background in the method. Using field diagrams, two of the decisions are analyzed as examples of the results of "give and take." In both cases, the concept that was finally agreed upon was at the intersection of the line of polarization and the line of balance, however the decisions differed in their level of creativity. The decision to refer to South West Africa as a geographical entity rather than as a State, or as Namibia, simply postponed the issue until a later time. In contrast, the decision with regard to use of formally white hotels by blacks combined the interests of those who wished to maintain the system of having to obtain permits for hotels that wished to serve blacks and also those who wished to have the hotels open to all. The decision that combined ideas, at creativity Level 3, could be expected to hold longer than the one to avoid the issue, but not as long as a decision involving a concept at an even higher level of creativity.

During the unrest associated with a boycott of the Coloured schools in Cape Town, South Africa in 1980, violence erupted in the suburb of Elsies River as cars of passing motorists were stoned. A few policemen set a trap for stone throwers by driving up and down the main street in an unmarked van until some stones were thrown. At this point, the street and a section of the sidewalk became the stage on which the police enacted their "morality play." Two youths were killed. The same street was turned into the scene for a nonviolent demonstration by Coloured schoolchildren at the youths' funeral. The directors and protagonists among the police and the community members who favored violent confrontation were replaced with scholars who symbolized and enacted a nonviolent theme. Both the enactments of the police and the scholars were consciously staged, and both had the effects desired by their playwrights, directors, and protagonists.

In Port Elizabeth, South Africa, during a strike by the black workers of the Ford Motor Company in 1979, white management did not want to negotiate with the workers. Alan Lukens, then U.S. Counsul-General arranged a meeting at a local hotel—neutral territory. Mr. Lukens introduced creative suggestions at many points during the meeting when otherwise the proceedings would have foundered for lack of worker representatives, ideas for solutions to differences in opinions, food, or a way of presenting the results of the discussion in the form of a press release. A time line indicating the act-by-act development of the conference shows that the group moved from L to

A in the expected order, but then jumped to G, and had to return to I before concluding the procedings at the press conference that involved the Terminal L.

Notes

1. The description of the Turnhalle conference is based on material that formed part of a report to the Human Sciences Research Council of South Africa in a 1983 reported entitled "Conflict and conflict resolution in South Africa: A dramaturgical perspective." The report included a paper by A. Paul Hare and Max H. von Broembsen entitled "The use of consensus at the Constitutional Conference in South West Africa," presented at meetings of the Association for Sociology in Southern Africa, Maseru, Lesotho, June 1979. The account of the incident in Cape Town was also included in the 1983 HSRC report. The descriptions of the Cape Town and Ford Motor Company incidents appeared, without analysis, in A. P. Hare (ed.) *The Struggle for Democracy in South Africa: Conflict and Conflict Resolution*, Cape Town: University of Cape Town, Centre for Intergroup Studies, 1983.

2. "Indaba" is a Zulu word referring to a council or conference. It is also used in the sense of to discuss or worry about something. Schapera (1962: 181-185) includes a brief discussion of the process as it is used in the Chief's Council of the Bantu Speaking Tribes and in the Great Council in which any member of the tribe may participate. Hammond-Tooke (1975: 64-75) gives a more detailed description of the process in the Transkei, including the observation that when the chief was consulting his council "The main aspect discussed by the Chief and his confidants in private was whether the people were happy about the decision, and not, apparently, the decision itself. Consensus was all important" (1975: 67).

Chapter 6

Egyptians and Israelis at Camp David

A. Paul Hare

David Naveh

The Camp David summit meeting in September 1978 produced two important accords: the Framework for Peace in the Middle East and the Framework for the Conclusion of a Peace Treaty between Egypt and Israel. A number of books have been written by persons who were part of that meeting of Egyptians, Israelis, and Americans (Brzezinski, 1983; Carter, 1982; Dayan, 1981, Vance, 1983; and Weizman, 1981). The authors have been concerned with the day-to-day activities and their political implications. For a dramaturgical analysis of this event, we have supplemented the published material with interviews of participants from the Egyptian, Israeli, and American teams whose comments were not for attribution. The present chapter is based on three articles that deal with aspects of the group process at Camp David: the effects of staging, the phases in group development, and examples of innovative decisions that led to conflict resolution (Naveh and Hare, 1985; Hare and Naveh, 1984, 1985). As an introduction to the events at Camp David, we first give a brief day-by-day account of the activity.

Day by Day at Camp David

Day 1, Tuesday, September 5. President and Mrs. Carter welcomed President Sadat on his arrival at Camp David. Mrs. Sadat did not attend the conference. The Egyptian delegation included Deputy Prime Minister Hassan el-Tohamey, Foreign Minister Muhammad Ibrahim Kamel, Head of the President's Bureau Hassan Kameil, and Secretary of State for Foreign Affairs Botrous Ghali, as well as several senior officials of the Foreign Ministry and the Office of the President. After a brief meeting between Carter and Sadat they agreed to meet the next morning.

Prime Minister Menachem Begin arrived several hours later. Although Mrs. Begin had not accompanied him, she was scheduled to arrive that evening. The Carters welcomed Begin and the Israeli delegation, including the Foreign Minister, Moshe Dayan, the Defense Minister, Ezer Weizman, a Supreme Court Justice, Aharon Barak (the former Attorney General who had just been appointed to the bench), and several senior advisers.

In the afternoon, President and Mrs. Carter secured the agreement of both leaders on the text of an interfaith prayer for peace. After supper, Carter and Begin met for two and a half hours, because, unlike Sadat, Begin was eager to get down to work. The conversation, according to Carter, was "discouraging" because Begin presented the "old Israeli negotiating positions" and expressed his opinion that the negotiations would take a long time. Begin expected that, at most, the summit would result in a declaration of principles for peace negotiations. Carter made it clear that he wanted final decisions at Camp David and that he was going to put forward his position forcefully (Carter, 1982: 337). He also impressed upon Begin the "advantages of good rapport between him and Sadat" (Carter, 1982: 333).

Close to midnight, Carter met with the American Secretary of State Cyrus Vance, and the National Security Adviser Zbigniew Brzezinski, to discuss his meeting with Begin. Also in the American delegation were Under Secretary of State Harold Saunders, Middle East expert on the National Security Council staff, William Quandt, as well as the American ambassadors to Egypt and Israel, Herman Eilts and Samuel Lewis. Vice President Walter Mondale and Secretary of Defense Harold Brown participated in some of the proceedings as did several other members of the president's staff and administration.

As the host, President Carter decided on an informal tone for the meetings. The participants were encouraged to dress informally. Meals were served in a common dining hall, and between meals, food and drinks were served at all hours. For recreation, various sports facilities as well as rooms for viewing movies were available. The informal setting combined with the proximity of the living units made it easy to arrange formal and informal discussions.

Day 2, Wednesday, September 6. Carter met with Sadat in the morning. The U.S. President found himself in agreement with Sadat who "wanted a firm framework for a permanent peace, and was eager to deal with all specific issues" (Carter, 1982: 339). It should be noted that Sadat and the Egyptian delegation were apparently convinced that an agreement with Begin could not be worked out. They wanted to expose Begin's intransigence at Camp David in anticipation of subsequent American support of the Egyptian position (Eilts, 1980: 3). Sadat handed Carter a plan that outlined extreme demands for Israeli withdrawal, concessions, and reparations. He confided in Carter that he was willing to make concessions.

At 3 p.m., the first meeting of the three leaders took place. The opening discussion dealt with the scope of the issues to be considered. It was agreed that all controversial issues should be included and that the Americans might present ideas of their own at some stage. Most of the session was devoted to Sadat reading his plan out loud. Begin, at Sadat's urging, saved his response for the next meeting after he had a chance to discuss the Egyptian plan with his advisers. Although there was an underlying tension, the meeting ended in "good spirits."

The Israeli delegation met that night and heard a detailed account of the meeting from Begin. It was decided that Israel would request that the Egyptian plan would be taken back. The Israelis began drafting a counterproposal.

Day 3, Thursday, September 7. In the morning, Carter, Vance, and Brzezinski met with Begin, Dayan, and Weizman. They worked out a compromise to avoid a conflict with Sadat. Rather than request that the Egyptian plan would be taken back, it was agreed that Israel would declare it unacceptable. The Americans were pleased to have Dayan and Weizman accompany Begin because the Americans felt that the two were more committed to accomplishing an agreement than the Premier was. Dayan was considered very creative as he kept coming up with deadlock-breaking formulas. He was also considered to have some influence on Begin. Weizman was thought to have little rapport with Begin but his friendship with Sadat was considered useful.

Later that morning, Sadat, Begin, and Carter met in the study of Carter's cabin. The session was full of anger and accusations. Following an adjournment for lunch, the session was resumed. By the end of the afternoon, the conference appeared to be deadlocked. As Sadat and Begin were about to leave, Carter rose and blocked the door of his study until they had both agreed to give him one more day to produce a draft agreement.

Given the evident failure of the Sadat-Begin meetings and the danger of the consequent total collapse of the talks had they continued, Carter decided to separate the two. From then on Sadat and Begin did not meet. Carter and his team preferred to deal with Begin through Weizman, Dayan, and Barak, rather than directly. They found the members of the Israeli team more flexible and congenial than their chief. In the Egyptian case, the opposite was true. Sadat was flexible on many issues and receptive to changes, yet his associates were holding back.

Later that night, after a Marine drill show and a reception, Carter and his chief advisers met with Sadat and his delegation. The American president assured them that he agreed with their demands and that the Israeli settlers would leave the Sinai and that a satisfactory solution to the Palestinian problem should be worked out. In general, throughout the summit, Carter was more in sympathy with the Egyptian position and found it easier to hold discussions with Sadat than with Begin. Although the Americans were meeting with the Egyptians, the Israeli delegation had a meeting to draft a counterplan.

Day 4, Friday, September 8. Carter operated with the knowledge that the Egyptians were seriously considering leaving. The American delegation met in the morning with the Israelis to report on the previous night with the Egyptians. In the afternoon, Carter met separately with Begin and Sadat. In his discussions with them, Carter emphasized the areas of agreement and the willingness of the other side to compromise. That evening the Carters and other members of the American delegation joined the Israelis in a high-spirited dinner and in singing to welcome the arrival of the Sabbath.

Day 5, Saturday, September 9. The Americans were busy preparing a draft proposal. The document was to cover more than fifty issues of controversy. The drafting was concluded by midnight. They decided to exclude the issues of the removal of Israeli settlements from the Sinai and a freeze on settlements in the other occupied territories. Because these were the major stumbling blocks, the Americans wanted to present them once the other issues were resolved. Carter noted that fatigue was taking its toll. Dinner that night was a festive occasion with special foods and entertainment.

Day 6, Sunday, September 10. Egyptian and Israeli delegations joined Carter for a six-hour tour of the Civil War battlefield at Gettysburg. At that time, several members of the Israeli delegation were busy drafting a press release that would explain to the world why the Camp David peace talks had failed. However, this "white paper" and those prepared by the other delegations never had to be used.

In the late afternoon and again through the late evening until 3 a.m., Carter, Mondale, Vance, and Brzezinski of the American delegation met Begin, Dayan, Weizman, and Barak of the Israeli delegation to go over the first American draft. Many of the major points in the proposal were debated heatedly. Carter had to postpone meeting Sadat until the next day. The Israelis acceded to Carter's request to wait for a revised version of the American proposal rather than introduce an Israeli draft. After the meeting, Carter took a walk with Dayan to discuss some of the pertinent issues.

Day 7, Monday, September 11. Carter met Sadat to discuss the American proposal that now included revision based on Israeli ideas with which Carter agreed. The Sinai settlements were still an issue as was the disposition of Jerusalem. Sadat took the document to confer with his advisers.

Later that day, Carter met Weizman and his aide, General Tamir, to learn about the military arrangements they had worked out with the Egyptians prior to Camp David. Meanwhile Vance and Eilts met with the Egyptians who expressed strong reservations about the American proposal. Carter had a meeting with Dayan and Barak.

Day 8, Tuesday, September 12. The negotiations seemed to be headed for a breakdown. Sadat had a rough meeting with his senior advisers. They were very critical of the American proposals and unhappy with the direction of the talks. Later than morning, Sadat met Carter. Sadat seemed very troubled throughout the meeting (Carter, 1982: 385). However, the meeting between Vance, Brzezinski, Dayan and Barak made some progress. Given these results, Carter proceeded to draft an agreement on the Sinai that he presented to Sadat three hours later. Sadat approved it.

Still more difficulties were presented to Carter as he met with Begin after supper with the Israeli delegation. The Israeli Premier expressed his firm opposition to including in the agreements the clause from UN Resolution 242 concerning the "inadmissibility of acquisition of territory by war." He also vowed that the Sinai settlements would not be given up. Begin offered Carter two forms of statements to end the summit. One would simply state the gratitude of Israel and Egypt for being invited to Camp David. The alternative statement would list the areas of agreement and disagreement. A discussion that Carter described as "heated . . . unpleasant and repetitive" followed. It ended with mutual accusations without any substantive results (Carter, 1982: 386-387).

Day 9, Wednesday, September 13. Carter decided to try a different way to break the deadlock on the negotiation of the Israeli-Egyptian framework. At his request, Sadat designated Osama el-Baz and Begin designated Aharon Barak to work on the language of the framework together with the American president and the secretary of state. They worked for eleven hours and made significant progress. After the meeting was over, Carter walked over to Begin to thank him for "the Israelis' constructive attitude during the day" (Carter, 1982: 388).

That night Carter could not fall asleep because he was concerned for Sadat's safety. Carter had been told earlier in the evening that he could not see the Egyptian president because he had retired earlier than usual. Carter feared that Sadat had been killed by one of his pro-PLO aides. In the middle of the night, Carter summoned to his cabin Brzezinski and the chief of security and ordered the strengthening of security around Sadat's cabin.

Day 10, Thursday, September 14. Carter joined Sadat's fast-paced morning walk. Sadat accepted several of Carter's proposals concerning Eilat and Jerusalem. The rest of the day was devoted to Israeli-American discussions on the Israeli-Egyptian accord. Barak and el-Baz continued to work on the language of the proposals. Towards the end of the day, there was a feeling that an agreement on all the issues could not be worked out. Discussions followed on how to make the anticipated breakdown appear as constructive as possible.

Day 11, Friday, September 15. Carter decided that the conference would end on the coming Sunday and informed Begin and Sadat. As Carter's staff was busy drafting his speech to Congress explaining the failure to reach an agreement at Camp David, the Americans were told of Sadat's intention to leave immediately. Apparently, following a meeting with Dayan, Sadat was angered by Dayan's statement that no Israeli government could evacuate the Sinai in less than five years (Eilts, 1980: 5). On hearing the news, Carter asked to be left alone and spent some time praying for an agreement. Afterwards he went over to see Sadat and in a moving conversation he convinced Sadat to stay on to the end. Later that evening, Carter and Mondale paid a social call on Sadat. Following a discussion of the framework, they watched the Ali-Spinks heavyweight boxing championship match on television.

Day 12, Saturday, September 16. The main obstacle to an agreement was overcome. Early in the day Sadat made it absolutely clear that he would not tolerate Israeli settlements in Sinai. Later, in a meeting with the Americans, Begin indicated that he had changed his position and was now willing to let the Knesset make the decision concerning the evacuation of the settlements. As a result, the road to agreement seemed open. Given the Sunday deadline, they rushed through the remaining issues, mainly those dealing with the West Bank and Gaza section of the Framework.

Day 13, Sunday, September 17. The framework for Peace in the Middle East and the Framework for the Conclusion of a peace treaty between Egypt and Israel was signed by Prime Minister Begin and President Sadat with President Carter as a witness. Yet, until the agreements were signed after 10 p.m., it was not clear that they would be signed after all. In the morning, although Sadat accepted the draft, a crisis developed over the question of Jerusalem. The Israelis objected to an American letter to Egypt, appended to the agreement, restating the American position that East Jerusalem was an occupied territory. After hectic negotiations throughout the day, a compromise was hammered out. In the midst of the crisis, Carter went over to Begin's cabin to personally deliver autographed pictures of the principals at the summit. The exchange between them was rather emotional "about grandchildren and about the war" (Carter, 1982: 399). Begin then expressed his sorrow that an agreement could not be worked out as he could not give in on Jerusalem. Some time later, he accepted an alternative draft that restated the positions of the three participants. Toward the end, some issues of language still kept the negotiators busy. As everyone was preparing to leave for the signing ceremony in Washington, it became known that the Egyptian Foreign Minister had resigned over the agreements. Most of the members of the Egyptian delegation were unhappy with the agreement and boycotted the ceremony.

As noted earlier, in the brief account of the activities on each day, the meetings that involved Carter have been stressed because he was the principal driving force behind the negotiations. Brzezinski (1983: 270-271) observed that "this was indeed his success. He was the one who gave it the impetus, the extra effort and the sense of direction." Throughout the summit, there were other meetings between each of the three principals and their delegations for briefings and discussions of the various drafts. There were also numerous formal and informal contacts between the various delegations.

Effects of Staging

We now turn to the first part of our analysis of the events at Camp David. Four aspects of the staging are considered: the space available within the grounds and structure at the camp, the scenery that provided a backdrop, the fact that the conference was being held "backstage" as far as the world public was concerned, and the relatively short time available for the work of the conference.

Space

The physical space of Camp David is 125 acres of wooded, mountainside grounds surrounded by a security fence. Sleeping cabins, a dining room, a swimming pool, tennis courts, and other sports facilities are spread within this space.

President Carter believed that holding the summit at Camp David would improve the interpersonal relationship between Begin and Sadat. Carter was convinced that "there was no prospect for success if the two men stayed apart and their infrequent meetings had now become fruitless because the two men were too personally incompatible to compromise on the many difficult issues facing them" (Carter, 1982: 316). President Carter hoped that at Camp David "both Begin and Sadat would come to trust me to be honest and fair in my role as mediator and active negotiator" (Carter, 1982: 322).

The fact that Begin and Sadat stayed in two cabins several hundred yards apart for thirteen days did not draw them closer. On the contrary, their mutual meetings together with Carter at the opening of the summit brought the talks to the verge of a total breakdown. According to one of the American participants, one of the Israelis came to see him after the third meeting between Begin and Sadat and asked to pass a message on to President Carter. The message was that in order to save the summit Begin and Sadat should be kept apart as the chemistry between them was bad. The Israeli also indicated that his team was writing a response to Sadat's extreme demands presented to Begin at their first meeting. He expressed his opinion that once the Israeli reply was presented the talks would break down. He urged the Americans to come up with their own proposal. The message was passed on to Carter. Whether influenced by this message or having reached this conclusion independently, President Carter proceeded to stop the meetings between the two chiefs and instructed members of his staff to prepare an American draft.

The story above can serve as an example of how the small space of Camp David made a significant impact on the conduct of the talks. Practically all people involved stayed a few yards apart from each other, ate in a common dining room, and ran into each other in the pathways of the camp. They could easily get from one part of the camp to the other by foot, bicycle, or golf-cart. The internal telephone could also be used although monitored by an American switchboard operator. All these facilitated rapid and continuous interaction among the participants. The ease of communication became even more important once the burden of improvising the agreements was passed down from the chiefs to their staffs. As one of the American delegates summed it up, "there was a great deal of interaction among the participants. Such speed of communication could not be achieved elsewhere. It had a quality which could not be replicated."

The intense interaction did not involve all the channels of communication. There was very little formal or informal direct contact between the Israelis and the Egyptians. Most of their communication was through American intermediaries. Israeli Defense Minister, Ezer Weizman, was the exception in his relations with the Egyptians, especially his meetings with Sadat.

The amount of interaction within the delegations was also intense. Living accommodations of 3-4 persons in a cabin created many opportunities for people to see and talk to each other. That helped subgroups of the various delegations to be in practically constant contact. Besides, each delegation held several meetings daily, in various subgroups, having to do with issues and personal relations.

In sum, the effect of the space of Camp David was not what Jimmy Carter had hoped. Neither did it help Begin and Sadat get close to each other nor did it promote relationships between the Israelis and Egyptians. However, the compactness of the camp contributed to the pace of the negotiations and to the ability to solve problems as they emerged. It allowed for the easy convening of meetings and for numerous informal and spontaneous encounters. On a more profound level, the close physical proximity of the participants and their intense interaction would not let people escape dealing with the problems. From a dramatic perspective, the space contributed to the intensification of life processes—a helpful element in a process of improvisation.

Scenery

In the scenery, we include the visual appearance of Camp David and its immediate surroundings, as well as the staff and services provided there. We also include the implicit and explicit rules guiding the interaction among the participants. Much of what will be said about the scenery complements what was said above about space.

President Carter had high hopes that together with the physical closeness the scenery of the Camp David summit would enhance the peace talks:

> Camp David is truly beautiful with the cottages (all named after trees) and paths snuggled on top and down one side of a small mountain and sheltered by a thick growth of stately oak, poplar, locust, hickory, and maple trees. A security fence encompasses about 125 acres of rocky terrain, and the close proximity of the living quarters engenders an atmosphere of both isolation and intimacy, conducive to easing tension and encouraging informality (Carter, 1982: 324).

To further develop that desired atmosphere, certain arrangements and rules were introduced that would be called "loosening up activities" for a dramatic improvisation (Hodgson and Richards, 1974). It was decided that all participants would eat in a common dining room. Snacks and beverages were available 24 hours a day. Those persons who wanted to could play tennis, swim, or take part in a variety of other sports. They could also participate in less physically active recreations such as shooting pool, playing chess, or watching a movie. Informality was accepted as the rule of behavior. It had to do with the dress code (the President wearing blue jeans) as well as with relating to other participants (if you wanted to talk to somebody, you could just walk over and do it). To use Burke's concept (1968: 446), President Carter was hoping for the proper "ratio" between the relaxed atmosphere and the conduct of the negotiations.

The short distances did not draw Begin and Sadat to each other, neither did the scenery. Much to Carter's disappointment, the beauty of the camp and its intimate and informal atmosphere had no effect on their feelings for each other. Furthermore, neither Sadat nor Begin subscribed to the rules of informality. Each kept to his own meticulous dress code. Begin, who at times made the concession of being seen without a tie, always insisted on dressing up for meetings with the U.S. President. Further, Begin occasionally would eat in the common dining room. Sadat never did. Both men stayed in their cabins most of the time. However, President Carter met with both chiefs frequently. He felt free to just walk over to their cabins whenever necessary.

With regard to the rest of the participants, the scenery complemented the space. Within the boundaries of the camp, the eating arrangements, the recreational amenities, and the code of informality further contributed to the scope and intensity of the negotiations. However, it is the opinion of the participants interviewed for this research that the pleasant atmosphere did not have a bearing on the substance of the negotiations. As one of them put it, "nobody was giving away anything over cocktails."

Backstage

In a play, the proportions and relationships among onstage, backstage, and offstage areas are important. Within a given space and scene at any time, the action can take place either onstage where it is seen by the audience or backstage where the actors prepare to go on stage or unwind. The offstage area includes the spectator area and other parts of the environment that are relevant to the progress of the play.

President Carter's decision to hold talks away from the public eye meant that they would be backstage as far as the world audience was concerned. Carter's main fear was that public statements would put the participants in "frozen positions which could not be subsequently changed" (Carter, 1982: 318). Carter reports that his "most difficult arguments" were with his media people who felt that, as a result, Carter would lose potential political benefits to his public image (Carter, 1982: 317-318).

Most members of both Israeli and American delegations were unanimous that closing off the summit from the outside world in general, and from the media in particular, was essential to the success of the talks. On the personal level, the news blackout prevented people from being publicly committed to a given position, as Carter expected. The lack of public statements by the participants allowed them to be flexible and, at times, creative without losing face. This was especially significant for the Israeli delegation. While the talks were in progress, Begin and the others did not have to contend with pressures from back home. As the Israeli public was not informed about the concessions being made at the summit, there were no objections voiced. The speculations published in the media were rather pessimistic, so that the fierce opposition that arose once the agreements became known was still dormant. A member of the American delegation summed this point up in a succinct way:

> The most important aspect was the privacy and isolation from the press and the outside world. Based on our experience in other negotiations with these two parties, considerable interaction with the press would have produced feedback from back home. Particularly in the case of the Prime Minister, it would have frozen him in a way he would have been unable to make any significant compromises.

In the case of the Egyptians, the news blackout was particularly useful in stopping the exchange with the Arab world as the talks were going on. There was not much to worry about from the Egyptian media because it was mostly government controlled. Yet Sadat, although he withstood Arab objections since his visit to Jerusalem, might have been influenced by additional pressures. This could have been combined with the pressures from members of his delegation, culminating in the resignation of his foreign minister before the end of the summit. He was particularly vulnerable to criticism of his allowing the Palestinian issue to be subdued. A tougher stand by the Egyptians on the West Bank might have brought about the breakdown of the talks.

Time

Especially in an improvisation, the amount of time allowed for the production affects the end product. President Carter underestimated how long it would take to work out an agreement:

> Our plans called for three days, but we were willing to stay as long as a week if we were making good progress and success seemed attainable. We never dreamed we would be there through thirteen intense and

discouraging days, with success in prospect only during the final hours
(Carter, 1982: 322).

When he saw that by the first weekend, no progress was made, he
decided to extend the conference without setting a specific time limit.
Towards the end of the second week, he set Sunday as the final
deadline. Still, throughout the summit, it was clear that it could end
any time. The participants realized that the U.S. President could not
stay forever. Ezer Weizman, for instance, was convinced that "Carter
and his men would operate a steamroller to push Sadat and Begin to
some conclusion. How long can you hold the U.S. President in the
'golden cage' of Camp David?" (Weizman, 1981: 317). An American
delegate agreed: "the longer we stayed, the greater was the pressure
to come up with some document."

Aside from the effect of the total time on the participants and their
perceptions of what was expected of them, the allocation of time
among the various subjects affected the substance of the agreement.
As members of the American delegation pointed out, there was a
preoccupation with the Sinai evacuation and the fate of the settlements
there for most of the time. That influenced the detail and precision
that could be attained on the Palestinian issue. The Americans
believed this was a deliberate strategy on the part of Menachem
Begin; as one of them put it: "Begin was very clever to delay dealing
with Judea and Samaria issues to the last few days. As a result the
phrasing of this part of the agreement was rather vague and towards
the end people were pressured to bring about a solution."

Another aspect of the time element was the fact that all those
confined to Camp David were separated from their everyday respon-
sibilities and families (only Carter and Begin brought their wives
along). They were all available for the negotiations 24 hours a day. It
was very unusual that these heads of states could devote all their time
to a single issue and forego their busy schedules.

From a different perspective, the intensity and brevity of the
discussions cancelled many influences that might have occurred had
the process been on a longer time span. The thirteen days at Camp
David put the Israeli-Egyptian negotiations in a "time capsule."
Prolonged negotiations over months and years are typically affected
by what happens to the actors and the world around them. Leaders
may lose their power (or even their lives—as in Sadat's case), people
may change their minds, political coalitions may reform, and so on.
At Camp David, the negotiations were completed in such a brief time
span that such influences were practically eliminated.

Phases in Group Development

For this part of our analysis we will consider the event in terms of
the functional theory of group development, outlined in Chapter 1,
which hypothesizes that groups usually develop through four major
phases or acts of providing values (L), resources (A), norms (I), and
leadership (G), with a terminal stage again of "L."

The activities at Camp David were not those of a single small group
whose members met together for a series of meetings that might easily
be classified according to the stages in group development. Rather the
activity was carried on within and among three national delegations
and their supporting staffs. However, all of the participants were at
Camp David to implement the same goals so that it is possible to
consider all of those present as constituting a single group with the
three delegations and the other smaller groups that were formed in the
process as subgroups. The three leaders, Carter, Sadat, and Begin,
formed the central subgroup. Although this subgroup was only active
during the first few days at Camp David, all of the other subgroups
worked to help accomplish the task that only the three leaders could
carry out: the signing of the frameworks for peace in the Middle
East.

The sessions at Camp David were not the first time that representatives of Egypt, Israel, and the United States had met to work on a
draft of an acceptable peace agreement and they would not be the last.
Negotiations had already been carried on through various forms of
summits, shuttle diplomacy, and conferences at the ministerial level
for about a year. As a result, all three sides had considerable experience in dealing with the issues and with each other.

The summit at Camp David was convened as an "all out" effort of
the American president to save the peace process. In his view, the
impasse in the negotiations in the summer of 1978 might have led not
only to a serious blow to Sadat's regime but also to a new war in the
Middle East.

Functional Analysis of Group Development at Camp David

As a first step toward the analysis of the phases of group development during the talks at Camp David, the total period of 13 days was
divided into natural time periods. Like the acts and scenes in a play,
the beginnings and endings of these natural time periods are indicated

by changes in the theme, the actors, or the setting. In this case our own estimates of the natural time periods were supported by asking the participants whom we interviewed what phases they could identify and what characterized the activity during each of these phases. By this method, five natural time periods were identified:

(1)   Days 1-3 when Carter held joint talks with Sadat and Begin.
(2)   Days 4-8 when Carter and his team were producing the American draft of the proposals consulting separately with Sadat and Begin and their advisers.
(3)   Days 9 and 10 when the drafting group featuring Barak and el-Baz was working on the details of the Egyptian-Israeli agreement with the Americans shuttling between the parties.
(4)   Days 10 and 11 when the parties were unable to overcome the Sinai issues culminating in the crisis and Sadat then prepared to leave.
(5)   Days 12 and 13 when solutions were found for the remaining problems and the Camp David accords were signed at the White House.

During the 13-day period Carter introduced festive meals, a Marine Corps drill, a trip to the Gettysburg battleground, and various other diversionary activities designed to reduce tension and allow participants to meet socially. However, there is no evidence in this case that any of the periods of recreation should be highlighted by considering it a separate phase. Although some of the delegates had especially friendly relationships both within and between delegations, most of these such as Carter-Sadat and Weizman-Sadat appear to have been made during the negotiations prior to Camp David. Throughout the summit meeting the small space, informal setting, and informal code of behavior did facilitate the interaction between the delegates.

In terms of functional theory, part of period 1 and periods 2 and 3 are similar in that they are each concerned with problems of "adaptation," as will be indicated below. They can be seen as a set because they are similar in theme but have a different task group as the major theme carrier and a different level of detail of the activity. Although not singled out by the participants interviewed for this study, the Carter-Being meeting the first evening and the Carter-Sadat meeting of Day 2 were concerned with the functional problem of pattern maintenance, because it was during this time that the three had to agree on their reason for coming to Camp David. The culmination of the talks in the White House signing ceremony should also be treated as a separate period as this was not only the actual "goal attainment" for the conference, but it was also held on a different stage and before an audience. Although as we shall note there was usually more than one scene within an act or period, overall, the group developed in the expected order of L-A-I-G.

Given the amendments to the natural time periods identified by the participants, the development at Camp David can be divided into seven acts as follows:

Act 1—Day 1 and the morning of Day 2: The activity was primarily in the "L" area as Carter discussed the overall purpose of Camp David with Sadat and Begin separately. The participants had held different ideas about the purpose of the summit before they arrived at Camp David. Carter established that his definition of the purpose would prevail. In this initial act, and on through the second act, Sadat and Begin were acting primarily in the antagonistic roles of heads of states rather than as negotiators.

Act 2—The afternoon of Day 2 and Day 3: Carter, Sadat, and Begin began the first of four "A" phases as they worked on a draft of the documents. Given that the eventual goal was to sign the "accords," two "frameworks" had to be constructed, one for Peace in the Middle East, and the other for the conclusion of a peace treaty between Israel and Egypt. In this case, the gathering of facts necessary for this construction constituted activity in the A area. However in this first act, Sadat and Begin as major theme carriers for their countries were unable to agree on a text. The act ended as Carter blocked the door to his study until they agreed to stay at Camp David to give him one more day to produce a draft. The threat that Sadat and Begin would leave posed a major problem for the conference and threw it back to the L stage again as a new commitment was required.

Act 3—Days 4-8: This is the second of the A phases as the American team worked on a draft. The act also ended in a crisis with a return to L as Sadat was "troubled" and Carter thought he was ready to leave. Begin proposed that they end the meetings and suggested a draft statement for the press. Carter again had to motivate Sadat and Begin to stay long enough for one more try.

Act 4—Day 9 through the afternoon of Day 10: This was the third session of A activity with Barak and el-Baz doing much of the work, accompanied by Carter and Vance.

Act 5—Evening of Day 10 and Day 11: Because Sadat insisted that the settlements be removed from the Sinai and Begin wanted to leave them there, Carter concluded that there was a deadlock and prepared to end the conference. This meant that the A activity had again failed to reach the final objective and the group was moved to the terminal L stage because there seemed to be no hope of completing the A stage and passing on through the I and G stages. Carter drafted a proposal for a final statement and press release as an activity for the final L stage. However, Sadat and his team packed their bags to leave, throwing the conference back to the initial L again. Carter once more had to motivate Sadat and Begin to stay until Sunday for closure.

Act 6—Days 12 and 13: During act 6, two types of activity were going on at the same time. As the curtain rose, most of the participants were preparing their final statements to describe the failure. But as Carter checked the list of points on which there was agreement, he did not give up hope and pressed to find a resolution to the issues of the settlements and Jerusalem. This was the fourth period of A superimposed upon the Terminal L phase. The breakthrough on the settlement issue, of having Begin refer the issue to the Israeli Knesset, was actually mentioned as a possibility on Day 7 by Dayan and Barak but not used. This shift of roles is an activity in the I area. It would seem that by declaring that a decision could not be reached, pressure was taken off so that people could think twice. Although actually Carter was pressing both Sadat and Begin very hard to find some agreement on the last few points. Fine changes in wording were necessary before agreement could be reached, for example, on the issue of the "self-government" of the Palestinians. As major theme carriers throughout the conference, Begin, Sadat, and Carter to a lesser extent, were very sensitive to any words or actions that would not fit the images they wished to project of their respective countries.

Act 7—Evening of Day 13: The final signing (G phase) took place. As noted above, in addition to a different functional content, this act is set apart because it is the only one that took place before an audience. Acts 1-6 took place backstage as the actors improvised and rehearsed their parts for the final performance. After the White House "opening," the show still had to go on the road to gain approval in Israel, Egypt, and the USA. There was hope that the "spirit of Camp David" (the illusion) would carry forward to solve the remaining problems of the occupied territories and of Jerusalem.

Although the analysis above was begun to test the hypothesis that the problem solving at Camp David would progress through the stages L-A-I-G, the actual "road to agreement" turned out not to be a wide, well-marked highway but a narrow, hazardous route with many switchbacks that brought the group time and again to the starting point. Although progress through the four stages was eventually achieved, the pattern of acts and scenes took the following form: Act 1 (L), Act 2 (A-L), Act 3 (A-L), Act 4 (A), Act 5 (Terminal L-L), Act 6 (Terminal L-A-I), and Act 7 (G).

Creativity in Conflict Resolution

As we have seen in the analysis of group development, the parties were wide apart on many issues during the intense 13 days of negotiations. Creativity on the part of the participants was required at various junctures in the talks to prevent breakdown or to regain momentum. For the analysis of creativity in conflict resolution, we make use of the distinction represented in Figure 1.1 between "social-emotional" behavior that usually focuses on the composition of the group and the relationships between members and "task" behavior that focuses on the problem-solving process.

In the social-emotional area, President Carter is credited with having the greatest influence on the changes in group composition that allowed the negotiations to move from a stalemate in the first few days to a period of creativity in the second week. During the first two days, Carter met for three sessions alone with Sadat and Begin. However, when it became clear that both of the principal parties were bringing the talks to the verge of breakdown, Carter introduced an American draft of a peace agreement, drawing on a document that had been prepared beforehand in case it was needed. The draft started circulating, bouncing back and forth between the delegations. By the time the final agreement was reached, it had gone through 23 drafts. When on the ninth day the drafting process seemed to run into difficulties, President Carter created a special drafting team including Israeli and Egyptian legal experts, Aharon Barak and Osama el-Baz, to work with him and Secretary Cyrus Vance. It was through this effort that solutions to some of the most pertinent issues were found. This was the turning point in the negotiations. Although the most difficult issues were left to the end, the momentum created by this drafting team was important for a successful completion of the summit.

In the task area, Carter pressed the delegates to consider the points on which they could more easily agree and leave the more difficult items until the end. He also introduced a creative move by concentrating on the arrangement for the return of the Sinai, which was crucial for the peace between Egypt and Israel, and leaving the proposals for the occupied territories to be dealt with later on. The actual process of negotiation consisted of finding statements on which both sides could agree. This process was described by one of the participants as "extending the margins" of the initial ideas that were in conflict until some overlapping area of agreement could be produced.

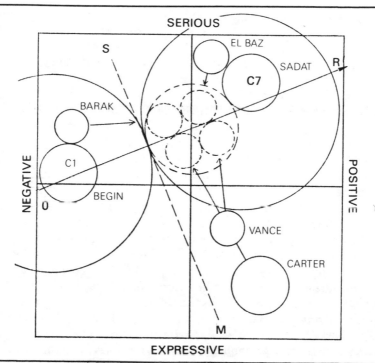

Figure 6.1   Social-Emotional Behavior of Participants When Egyptian Side Presented (during first days at Camp David)

Social-Emotional Creativity

President Carter's creativity in the social-emotional area is depicted in a field diagram in Figure 6.1. The diagram indicates the relative positions of Sadat and Begin when Sadat was presenting the Egyptian proposal during the first few days of the conference. To simplify the picture only the position of one member of the Egyptian delegation, el-Baz, is shown. The others would also be shown as serious, positive, and conforming, because they were acting in favor of the Egyptian proposals, even though they were not actually present during the Carter-Sadat-Begin dicussions. The position of Sadat is shown with a large circle as he was the most dominant member of the Egyptian delegation.

Because the first proposal of the Egyptians was not satisfactory to the Israelis, their behavior at the time would be shown as generally serious, negative, and anticonforming. However, as before with the picture of the Egyptian delegation, only the position of one member of the Israeli delegation, Barak, is shown. Begin is shown as very dominant because he was representing the Israeli disagreement with the Egyptian proposal.

Carter and the members of his delegation, represented here by Vance, had a position between the Egyptian and Israeli delegations in the positive direction.

Following Bales's method for the analysis of a field diagram, two large circles are placed in the diagram in such a way that all or most of the smaller circles, representing the positions of the group members, fall inside one or the other of the circles. If all of the positions of the members were contained within one of the circles, the group would be described as "unified." However, as in this case, if some of the members are in one circle and the others in the second circle, then the group is described as "polarized." The solid line passing through the centers of the two large circles with an arrow on the forward-positive end is the "line of polarization," indicating the direction of the polarization within the group. The arrow-tipped end of the line is labelled "R" to indicate the "reference direction." In this diagram, the behavior of the Egyptian side is taken as the reference direction because they are presenting. The behavior of the Israeli delegation is at the other pole, marked "O" for the "opposite direction." When the Israeli proposal was being presented by Begin, the behavior of the two sides would be reversed. The reference direction would be the same, but now the Israeli behavior would be shown as forward and positive.

The dashed line in Figure 6.1, passing between the two circles at right angles to the line of polarization, is the "line of balance." The righthand end is labelled "M" for "mediator direction" and the lefthand end, "S" for "scapegoat direction." As indicated in Chapter 1, polarized groups can be unified in three ways: (1) by a mediator who tends to take a position that is positive and midway between the two poles, where he or she can present images that draw the polarized individuals to a common positive identity, (2) by a scapegoat (a person, group, or idea) that is seen to be hostile to all the members so that they can become unified by being against the scapegoat, or (3) by domination of the two polarized sections and "knocking their heads together" in the interest of a common cause.

In the case of Camp David, rather than attempt any one of these three methods with Sadat and Begin, Carter reorganized the conference so that the primary work was done by a "drafting group" composed of one member of the Egyptian delegation (el-Baz) and one member of the Israeli delegation (Barak) with Carter and Vance sitting in as third parties.

The effect was to exclude the two most dominant members at the conference and compose a small group that had a greater potential for behavior that was serious (task oriented) lawyers' negotiation, without being too positive or too negative, and where neither the Egyptian nor the Israeli would be too upward (dominant). In this small group (represented by the dashed circle in the figure), Carter was the dominant member, and thus can be seen as using some domination as an additional technique for unification.

Carter's choice of el-Baz and Barak as the particular members of each delegation to do the work was also a creative move. Both were lawyers and thus had a common background as well as experience in working with legal documents. In addition, el-Baz was known to be more "hard line" in his position regarding the Egyptian proposal than Sadat. Thus Carter thought that anything that seemed fair to el-Baz would also obtain Sadat's approval. On the other side, Barak was believed to have much influence over Begin. Thus anything that seemed fair to Barak had a good chance of eventually being approved by the Prime Minister (Carter, 1982: 387). Both el-Baz and Barak would have had to change their behavior to take part in the new drafting group by playing professional roles rather than by being proponents of their own country's position. Both would have to move equal distances from their starting positions as members of opposing delegations. The new positions in the drafting group are indicated by the small circles within the dashed circle in Figure 6.1.

Task Creativity

The actual work in the task area of finding images of the kinds of future cooperation between Egypt and Israel for inclusion in the peace treaty between the two countries and their joint concern for a solution to the occupied territories of the West Bank, Gaza, and Jerusalem, is represented by the 23 revisions of the proposals that were drafted at Camp David before the final version was produced. As one example of the work, Figure 6.2 gives an indication of the way in which consensus was reached on a common image concerning the issue of who would guard the public order on the West Bank. Egypt wanted Jordon to supply arms and have a military presence on the

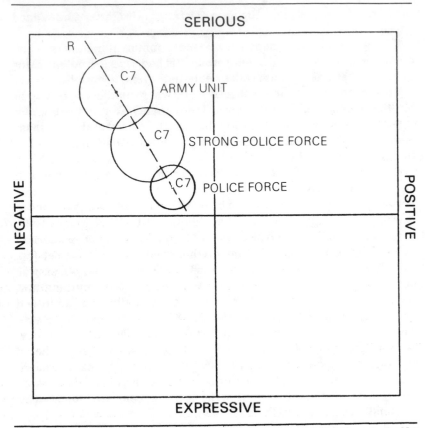

Figure 6.2   Images of Army Unit, Police Force, and Strong Police Force in the Negotiations Concerning West Bank

West Bank. This idea is plotted as a large circle (dominant image) in the serious-negative quadrant for Figure 6.2 (all of these ideas are highly conforming).

The Israelis agreed that there was a need for some security force on the West Bank, but could not agree to Jordanian troops. Also the ideas that Israeli troops would maintain order was a "nonstarter" as far as the Egyptians were concerned. The Israelis brought forward the idea of a local Arab police force (plotted as the smaller circle in the serious-negative quadrant of Figure 6.2). However the Egyptians were still not satisfied as they wanted a strong Arab presence in the area. So it was suggested that there be a "strong Arab police force." The adjective "strong" was important for the Egyptians but not for the Israelis. This can be seen, in Figure 6-2, as "extending the margins" by creating a new image of a strong police force that overlapped with both the initial image of a Jordanian army unit, put forward by Egypt, and the image of an Arab police force put forward by Israel.

In terms of the five levels of creativity identified by Taylor, this new concept of a "strong" police force is an example of an innovation at Level 4 (innovative). The idea of a strong police force was more than simply a combination of a concept of an army with a concept of a police force. Rather it provided an extension of the idea of a police force so that the new concept fell between that of an ordinary police force and a military unit.

In the previous example—Carter's creativity in finding a new combination of persons who would be able to reach agreement—the creativity was at Level 3 (inventive). Both el-Baz and Barak used interpersonal styles and problem solving skills that they already possessed and the idea of a "drafting group" was not new. Carter's ingenuity was in finding the right combination of persons to form the drafting group.

Summary

The events at the summit conference at Camp David in 1978 were summarized in a day-by-day account based on published records and interviews with participants. The space and scenery did not have the anticipated effect on the main actors nor did they bring about a relaxed and direct exchange between the negotiating parties. However, the intimate space and atmosphere helped to create an intense and productive process of improvisation: The summit participants improvised a mutually agreed on framework for peace in the Middle East. The scenery and the fact that the improvisation took place backstage might have helped create an artificial reality—an illusion—for those present, which put them in a state more favorable to the signing of an agreement. The thirteen days of the summit were long enough to allow the reaching of an agreement. Yet, they were short enough not to allow time for dwelling too long on "touchy" subjects as well as for creating a "time capsule."

The phases of group development during the 13-day period were analyzed from a functional perspective. The group progressed through the phases in the expected order, dealing in turn with problems of pattern maintenance, adaptation, integration, and goal attainment. However there were major crises on four occasions when either Sadat or Begin or both prepared to quit the conference, bringing the group back to the problem of pattern maintenance until Carter found a solution.

Two instances of creativity at Camp David, one in the social-emotional area, and one in the task area were analyzed using field diagrams to depict the images involved. In both cases, solutions were found that were near the intersection of the line of polarization and the line of balance in the field diagrams.

Appendix 1

Dramatism in Social Psychology

In Chapter 1, I have introduced some of the basic concepts that are used in the analysis of the case material on conflict and conflict resolution in Chapters 3-6. However there are many more concepts and hypotheses concerning the nature of social interaction as drama in the social psychological literature. This appendix provides a brief review of some of the work of persons who have made contributions to this perspective.

The Scene-Act Ratio

Anyone who wishes to trace the development of the dramaturgical perspective would do well to begin with the classic work of Kenneth Burke (1945). A summary of his ideas are presented in his article on "dramatism" in the *International Encyclopedia of the Social Sciences* (1968).[1] Here he describes the five key terms that philosophers have used to describe social interaction: act, agent, scene, agency (means employed by the agent), and purpose. To these he adds a sixth term: attitude. As Bales and Cohen do later in their SYMLOG approach (1979), he notes that the same act can be viewed from different system levels. A British author, he gives the example that an action at Number 10 Downing street can also have implications for Western Civilization.

Burke calls our attention to the importance of the stage and the scenery where an action occurs in setting limits on both form and content of the interaction. He calls this the "scene-act ratio." This fact helps understand the applause of a theater audience on those occasions when the curtain rises revealing the set but no actors. The time, place, and mood of the action is already implied by the set, be it comedy, tragedy, melodrama, or farce. Burke notes that:

> The stage-set contains the action *ambiguously* (as regards the norms of action) and in the course of the play's development, this ambiguity is converted into corresponding articulacy. The proportion would be: scene is to act as implicit is to explicit. One could not deduce details of the actions from the details of the setting, but one could deduce the quality of the action from the quality of the setting (Burke, 1945: 7).

Dramaturgical Perspective and Symbolic Interactionism

As has been mentioned in Chapter 1, some of the main contributions to the dramaturgical perspective have come from persons associated with the "Chicago School" and have been seen as a subtype of symbolic interactionism. Brisset and Edgley (1975: 2, 7) call attention to this fact in a book of readings entitled "Life as Theater." They suggest that the dramaturgical perspective can be summarized in nine principal characteristics:

(1) It is the study of meaningful behavior; meaning is viewed as problematic, arising in and through interaction.
(2) It views one's sense of individuality (one's self) as established, not reflected, in interaction.
(3) It views socialization as a process that furnishes the resources for situational variation, not as one that produces mechanisms for ensuring cultural uniformity.
(4) It rejects classical determinism; its method is prospective rather than retrospective.
(5) It is situationally, as well as culturally, relativistic.
(6) It views situations as defined interactionally, not mentalistically.
(7) It views the human being as fundamentally a communicator.
(8) It views interaction and situations, not individuals, as the locus of motivation.
(9) It views human beings as consciously rationalizing, not consciously rational.

These nine characteristics differ from the topics covered in the reader on symbolic interaction edited by Stone and Farberman (1981) in that the selections on socialization as a life process do not appear in the reader on the dramaturgical perspective. However the article by Maines (1981) in the Stone and Farberman reader casts a wider net in his review of recent developments in symbolic interactionism by including research on phenomenological sociology, labeling theory, sociolinguistics, interaction process, strategic interaction, and social organization.

In this text, there is no intention to leave out any of this material in the ultimate version of the dramaturgical perspective. Anything we know about social psychology tells us something about the ways in which persons prepare for and enact the social dramas of everyday life. Today there still seems to be some point in turning the spotlight on the dramatic aspect of social interaction. Tomorrow there may be enough social psychological illumination from different theoretical perspectives to be able to see all that needs to be seen.

If the task were only one of calling attention to the dramatic quality of much of everyday life, then it would be difficult to "upstage" the presentation of Lahr and Price (1973), who with words and many pictures have produced a book about the "life show" or "how to see theater in life and life in theater." However, social psychology as a science must not only have a point of view but also a method. Chapter 1 includes the main concepts, such as creativity, four dimensions of interaction, and four functions, for which some measures are already available. This appendix brings together some of the dramaturgical concepts in current use that could be operationalized for future analysis.

Drama, Real or Metaphor

Although much has been said about the concept of role, it is important to keep in mind that these roles are parts of plays. The plays in turn are composed of acts, and these of scenes, in which the actors dramatize the theme of a plot. Because there are occasions when persons in the roles of actors mount a stage to enact a play, the term "play," as it is used to describe events in everyday life, is being used by some social psychologists as a metaphor. For example, Sarbin (Allen and Scheibe, 1982) who has contributed much to the analysis of the part played by metaphor in social behavior, builds on the ideas of Pepper (1942) who identified six "world hypotheses" (animism, mysticism, formism, mechanism, contextualism, and organism). Each of these hypotheses is based on a "root metaphor" such as the idea that individual and group behavior is like a machine, or is like an organism. The contextual view is essentially the dramaturgical view. The root metaphor is the historical event (Allen and Scheibe, 1982: 19):

> The imagery called out by the historical event metaphor is that of an ongoing texture of multiply elaborated episodes, each leading to others each being influenced by collateral episodes, and by the efforts of multiple actors who perform actions in order to satisfy their needs and meet their obligations. Contained in the metaphor is the idea of constant change in the structure of situations and in the positions occupied by the actors. Linearity is not intended.

Sarbin cites the field theory of Lewin (1935) and the dramaturgical model of Mead (1934) and Goffman (1959) as being in this tradition. The emphasis here is on the possibility of conflicts of interest and change in human activity. Presumably this emphasis on historical events and on conflict as well as on roles is intended as a bridge between the conflict theorists on the one hand and the functionalists with a more static conception of role, on the other.

Burke (1968: 448) who (as noted in the opening lines of this appendix) also uses dramatism as a model for the analysis of social behavior argues that drama is *not* a metaphor, but the way symbolic interaction really occurs. He says that "drama is employed, not as a metaphor but as a fixed form that helps us discover what the implications of the term 'act' and 'person' *really are.*"

McCall (Stryker, 1981: 16) would agree that real life is drama. For him "identity, meaning, and social acts are the stuff of drama; as drama involves parts to be played, roles implicit in the parts must be conceived and performed in ways expressive of the role. The construction of social conduct involves roles and characters, props and supporting casts, scenes and audiences." MacCannell (1973: 10) makes a similar statement: "The structural principles which make what happens on the stage meaningful are the same as those which give meaning to everyday life."

For the present analysis, we take the view that there is a continuum ranging from everyday activities that do not have a dramatic quality, through social events that are consciously staged, to theater productions (see Chapter 2). In every case, the same social psychological variables are at work. However the playwrights, directors, actors, and critics involved with theater have paid considerable attention to some of the processes involved in the presentation of an idea to an audience. We can therefore turn to them for a source of concepts and hypotheses to be used until more exact terms can be derived (see Chapter 2).

Roles and Role Enactment

For Sarbin, role enactment (or social interaction) was the bridge between the individual and the group, between personal history and social organization. In his discussion of role theory, he provides a number of concepts that are useful in identifying the general aspects of roles (Allen and Scheibe, 1982: 37-57). Sarbin begins his observation about social behavior by asking questions about the appropriateness, propriety, and convincingness of the enactment of a role:

(1) Is the conduct appropriate to the social position granted to or attained by the actor? That is, do his performances indicate that the actor has taken into account the ecological context in which the behavior occurs? In short, has he selected the correct role?

(2) Is the enactment proper? That is, does the overt behavior meet the normative standards that serve as valuational criteria for the observer? Is the performance to be evaluated as good or bad?

(3) Is the enactment convincing? That is, does the enactment lead the observer to declare unequivocally that the incumbent is legitimately occupying the position?

Although these observations could be made about any type of role from the most formal roles in organizational settings to the more ephemeral roles that persons might take in some of Berne's games (1964), they would appear to be more easily applied at the formal end of the continuum.

Sarbin goes on to identify three dimensions of role enactment:

(1) The number of roles (played by an individual or in a group).

(2) Organismic involvement (the amount of effort put into the role).

(3) Preemptiveness (the relative amount of time a person spends in a role).

The other concepts that Sarbin finds useful in role analysis include the following:

- *Role expectation:* The rights and duties of a social position that is involved with complementary positions in a role set.
- *Role location:* A cognitive process by which the person determines "who is he?" and "who am I?" in terms of a role system.
- *Role demands:* The range of possible role behaviors required of a person in a given situation.
- *Role skills:* Physical and psychological readiness to perform some task to some given level of competence. Skills are both cognitive (taking the role of the other) and motoric (posture, movements, facial expression, and tone of voice).
- *Self-role congruence:* The self is the "experience of identity arising from a person's interbehaving with things, body parts, and other persons." Role enactment is more effective when self characteristics are congruent with role requirements.
- *Audience:* Role enactment is sometimes directed toward an audience (that may not be present, i.e. a reference group). Functions of an audience include the following:
  (a) Establishing consensual reality for the role.
  (b) Providing cues to guide the performance.
  (c) Giving social reinforcement.
  (d) Contributing to the maintenance of role behavior over time since the actor is continually observed.
- *Complex role phenomena:* Actors may play several roles at one time or several persons may play the role. This opens opportunities for varieties of role conflict such as when different groups or subgroups have different expectations for the same role, or a person tries to play different roles with incompatible expectations, or two or more role players have roles that collide [Hare, 1976: 148-150].

The lists given above do not exhaust Sarbin's contributions to role analysis nor those of others who have contributed to the field. The lists are introduced as a "starter set." Other items and perspectives could easily be added.

With Blau, we could discuss "exchange theory" both as a way of describing how the "right and duties" of role are actually transacted and also the motivating factors that might lead a person to take on a new relationship (or role) and to leave an old one. Blau notes that the basic assumptions of social exchange are (1968: 452):

Men enter into new social associations because they expect doing so to be rewarding and that they continue relations with old associates and expand their interaction with them because they actually find doing so to be rewarding.

Redl (1965) provides a thematic interpretation of roles with emphasis on the fact that the person who is *central* to a group, in that the activity is focused on him or her, may not be a "leader" in the usual sense. Redl's ten types of central members are described in psychoanalytic terms as those who act in the service of the id, the ego, the ego ideal, or the super ego.

Berne (1964) has presented what appears at first to be a rather simple set of three possible roles: parent, adult, and child. He suggests that all persons no matter how young or old they may be, can remember the activities associated with a younger age, the *child*, those activities associated with the current age status, the *adult*, and those activities with the older, responsible person, the *parent*. There turn out to be a variety of types within each level of the hierarchy. In Berne's game terminology, some of the varieties of adult role include sulks, jerks, squares, todies, show offs, clings, and prigs.

Klapp called attention to the role of heroes, villains, and fools and the parts they played in sustaining or changing the American character. He noted that in everyday life people used stereotypes such as "jerk, eager beaver, good Joe, or playboy" to express approval or disapproval of what some Americans were doing (1962: 16). The heroes were followed, set up as models, and given a central part in dramas. Villains were negative models of evil to be feared and hated. Fools were negative models of absurdity to be ridiculed. Taken together, the heroes, villains, and fools represented three dimensions of deviation from the norms: (1) better than, (2) dangerous to, and (3) falling short of (Klapp, 1962: 17).

Several types of fools were observed (Klapp, 1962: 69):

(1)   Incompetents (clumsy, rash, simple, weak) who illustrate and penalize ludicrous role failures.

(2)   Types who discount people who claim more than they have, thus correcting certain status-abuses and pretensions.

(3)   Non-conforming types who ridicule deviants and outsiders.

(4)   Overconformers who suffer comic rebuke because they have been too enthusiastic in complying with group standards.

(5)   Certain types (especially comic butt, clever fool) having conspicuous functions as outlets for aggressive tension.

Klapp saw the heroes and villains as supporting characters in the same dramas. He grouped them according to the main theme as follows (1962: 66):

Hero Types	Corresponding Theme	Corresponding Villains
good Joes, charmers	belongingness and acceptability	strangers, isolates, monsters, false friends, deceivers
conformers (moralists, smoothies)	conformity	outlaws, rebels, flouters, corrupters
group servants (benefactors, defenders, martyrs)	cooperation and solidarity	shirkers, loafers, quitters, parasites, chiseler, traitors, cowards
winners (strong men, top dogs, brains, smart operators, great lovers)	getting what you want and competing against others fairly	selfish, grabbers, cheaters, bullies, cowards, authoritarians, oppressors, criminal masterminds con men, wolves

Because the situations in which persons find themselves change from time to time, and even from moment to moment, persons may need to change roles from one situation to the next, or even play several roles at the same time. Swanson (1968: 442) emphasized this changeability in review of the theory of symbolic interaction where he observes that in the tradition of G. H. Mead,

> Interpretations of social life as symbolic interaction conceived of actors as constantly establishing and re-establishing their mutual relations, modifying or abandoning them as the occasion demanded. Thus, social life was viewed as a process by which actors collectively solved problems, the nature and persistence of their solutions varying with the problems they defined.

Ralph Turner has made a similar point, with emphasis on the fact that persons continually check to see if the roles are appropriate for the situation.

> Actors will behave as though they and others with whom they interact are in particular roles as long as the assumption works by providing a

stable and effective framework for interaction. They test the assumption by continuously assessing one another's behavior, checking whether that behavior verifies or validates the occupancy of a position by corresponding to expectations and by demonstrating consistency [Stryker, 1981: 20].

Although the fact that the plot of the play in which our real life actors are taking part is continually changing may seem to make any form of meaningful analysis almost impossible, there turn out to be a limited number of dramatic situations. For example, Polti (1977), writing in the early 1900s, analyzed some 1,200 literary works and identified no more than 36 dramatic situations. This list can be further reduced to seven sets of situations in an analysis presented in Appendix 2. Folklorists have also provided classifications of fairy tales and legends.

A more contemporary list of plots is given by Berne in his book on "Games People Play" (1964). His list of plots includes life games, such as "Alcoholic," "Kick me," and "See what you made me do," marital games, such as "If it weren't for you,' and "Look how hard I've tried," party games, sexual games, underworld games, consulting room games, and good games.

With the introduction of comprehensive schemes for role analysis such as those of Bales (1970; Bales and Cohen, 1979) that has been described earlier, it should be possible to compare these various lists and reduce them to a fairly manageable set; however, to date the classification of plots and the classification of roles has generally been carried out in different fields by different persons.

Convention in the Theater and in Social Life

Elizabeth Burns has made an extensive analysis of the use of convention in the theater and in social life (1972). She draws on the insights of playwrights, directors, critics, and actors as well as social scientists concerning the nature of theatricality. She begins with the observation that people inhabit many social worlds, each of these, like the *illusion* in a staged play, is a construct arising from a common perspective held by the members of that world. In Thomas's terms, the participants hold a common definition of the situation from which the action follows (Volkart, 1951).

Illusion is only a specifically theatrical term for a process inherent in all social interaction. It is the process of confining attention to those involved in a specific situation, of limiting activities, given that situation, to what is appropriate or meaningful or consequential, and of observing a defined level of reality. The process is essentially that of providing a frame for action (Burns, 1972: 17).

The levels of reality in ordinary life are approximately the same as the three levels of reality that are commonly accepted in the theater: (1) the *pretend* reality of games, sports, parties, and ceremonies, (2) the *alternative* reality of occupational worlds and ritual, and (3) the *overriding* reality concerned with efforts to change or defend definitions of the situation (i.e. the rules of the game).

This continuum of levels of reality from *pretend* to *alternative* to *overriding* helps us repond to those critics of dramaturgical analysis of social interaction who point out that roles are fixed in the theater, but are constantly changing in real life. At the pretend reality end of the continuum the roles are relatively fixed, but at the overriding reality end, the roles are created at the moment. Using these three levels of reality as a base, we can also place some of the observations made by others using similar concepts. For example, Sarbin has described eight types of organismic involvement (effort) that he also identifies as levels (Allen and Scheibe, 1982: 40-44). The levels are as follows:

Zero — Noninvolvement
   I — Casual role enactment
  II — Ritual acting
 III — Engrossed acting
  IV — Classical hypnotic role taking
   V — Histrionic neurosis
  VI — Ecstasy
 VII — Bewitchment

An indication of the way in which these various concepts fit together is given in Figure A1.1. Here it is helpful to consider not only a range of behaviors that are unconsciously or consciously related to role, but also those behaviors that are unconsciously or consciously related to the self or personality. Whether the behavior is more closely related to role or to the self, what we observe in each instance is social interaction.

At the top of Figure A1.1 is a continuum for role behavior ranging from the least conscious, on the left, where the role is imposed without cooperation of the person, to the most conscious, on the right where

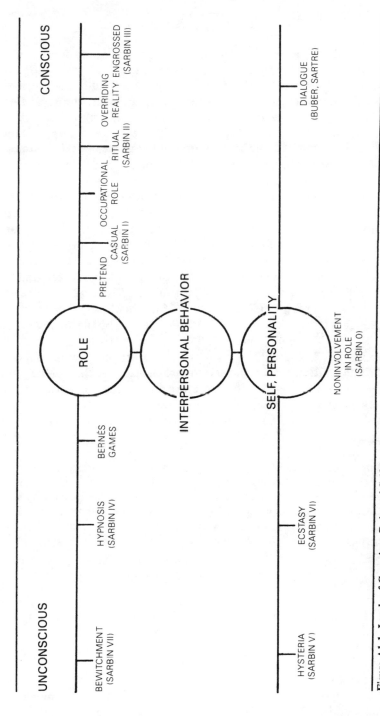

Figure A1.1 Levels of Conscious Role and Self-Involvement

153

the person is fully alive to the possibilities of maintaining or creating a role. Most of the discussion of roles in the social psychological literature deals with the righthand end of the continuum, as described by Burns, including the pretend, alternative, and overriding realities. Sarbin's first three levels of casual, ritual, and engrossed acting would seem to fit here at approximately the same points. On the unconscious end of the role continuum would fall many of the "games" that Berne describes, and Sarbin's levels IV and VII, classical hypnotic role-taking and bewitchment.

Sarbin's types V and VI seem to have a closer relationship to the self or personality than to a social role, thus they are placed on the unconscious end of the personality continuum, with histrionic neurosis probably being less of a conscious activity than ecstasy states. At the most conscious end of the self continuum would be the highly conscious interactions between the self and the other, represented by Buber's dialogue between I and Thou (Buber, 1970) and the absence of Sartre's "bad faith" (Caws, 1979: 76). This form of interaction that appears to be "self" to "self" would seem to be the same as that identified by Moreno as the "tele" relationship (two-way empathy) (Moreno, 1972: 238ff.). For professional actors, an attempt is made to reach this ultimate form through improvisation. Although the term "improvisation" is used in the literature on theater to describe many levels of creativity, the most conscious end of the self continuum is described by Peter Brook, a director with the Royal Shakespeare Company in England, as follows:

> Many [improvisation] exercises set out first to free the actor, so that he may be allowed to discover by himself what only exists in himself; next to force him to accept blindly external directions, so that by cocking a sensitive enough ear he could hear in himself movements he would never have detected in any other way. . . . Improvisation aims at bringing the actor again and again to his own barriers, to the point where in place of new-found truth he normally substitutes a lie. . . . If the actor can find and see this moment he can perhaps open himself to a deeper, more creative impulse [Smith, 1975: 80 ff.].

In the various discussions of reality the terms creativity, spontaneity, and involvement occur over and over again. As indicated in Chapter 1, the levels of reality and creativity in social action appear to be the same as the levels of creativity in artistic and scientific endeavor (Hare, 1982: 160ff.). The lowest levels involve acting with a set framework, the highest levels involve creating new frameworks and new understandings. In every case, the action begins with some understanding on the part of the participants about "what is supposed to be going on here" (Burns, 1972: 41). From this follows the set of characters, the plot, and the level of creativity in the enactment.

Self-Role Merger

Ralph Turner suggests that an understanding of the extent of the merger between self and role in any situation is important for an understanding of symbolic interaction (Stryker, 1981: 20-22). Turner observes that our self conceptions arise out of interaction with others, and we present ourselves to others in light of these self conceptions. In an instance of interaction, we seek both to infer the roles of others and to inform others of the nature of the role we are playing, and the role is consistent with and invested in the self.

The roles we play have two main goals, one to achieve group goals efficiently and the other to achieve personal reward in the form of validation of self, self-esteem, and reinforcement from others. People's ideas about their "real selves," that is about who and what they really are, depend on whether their ideas about themselves have an "institutional" emphasis or an "impulse" emphasis. If they have an "institutional" emphasis, people will see their real selves in feelings, attitudes, and actions that are anchored in institutions. They will recognize their real selves in action when accepting group obligations. On the other hand, people who have an "impulse" emphasis will see their real selves in untamed impulse with conformity to institutional norms occurring at the expense of their true selves. Turner suggests that over the past several decades there was a major shift in the locus of self in American society from institution to impulse.

The Presentation of Self in Everyday Life

Erving Goffman's volumes of close observation of incidents of social interaction in everyday life provide many examples of the similarities between ordinary behavior and the presentations of actors upon a stage (Goffman, 1959, 1961, 1963, 1967, 1968, 1970, 1972, 1974). Throughout, the emphasis has been on the way persons present themselves in roles in order to control both their own images and the overall themes of the interaction.[2] Most of the attention is given to microanalysis of informal encounters such as gatherings on the streets, in parks or in restaurants. When a formal organization is observed, such as a mental hospital, it is the "backstage" behavior of doctors, nurses, and patients that Goffman (1968) finds most interesting. The "strategic interaction" (calculated gamelike aspects of mutual dealings) of secret agents and spies provide examples of ways in which persons are able to structure a course of action that objectively alters the situation of the participants (Goffman, 1970).

Following the social interactionist tradition Goffman (1974) was interested in the impact of the situation on interpersonal behavior. He labeled his approach "frame analysis," calling attention to those aspects of the situation that would answer the question "What is going on here"? Any situation can be transformed through "keying" actions to one that has a different frame (that is a different definition of the overall image, theme, plot, or script). The major frames into which actual activity may be transformed are as follows: fun, deception, experiment, rehearsal, dream, fantasy, ritual, demonstration, analysis, and charity (Goffman, 1974: 560).

Team Work

Although there are many occasions when an individual is left to his or her own devices to save face and play out a role that is appropriate for the situation, there are also occasions when the individual has the support of others as part of a team. In his conclusion to the book on the presentation of self, Goffman summarizes this teamwork as follows (1959: 238-239):

> Within the walls of a social establishment we find a team of performers who cooperate to present to an audience a given definition of the situation. This will include the conception of own team and of audience and assumptions concerning the ethos that is to be maintained by rules of politeness and decorum. We often find a division into back region, where the performance of a routine is prepared, and front region, where the performance is presented. Access to these regions is controlled in order to prevent the audience from seeing back stage and to prevent outsiders from coming into a performance that is not addressed to them. Among members of a team we find that familiarity prevails, solidarity is likely to develop, and that secrets that could give the show away are shared and kept. A tacit agreement is maintained between performers and audience to act as if a given degree of opposition and accord existed between them. Typically, but not always, agreement is stressed and opposition is underplayed. The resulting working consensus tends to be contradicted by the attitude toward the audience

which the performers express in the absence of the audience and by carefully controlled communication out of character conveyed by the performers while the audience is present.

We may find that discrepant roles develop: some of the individuals who are apparently teammates, or audience, or outsiders acquire information about the performance and relations to the team which are not apparent and which complicate the problem of putting on the show. Sometimes disruptions occur through unmeant gestures, faux pas, and scenes, thus discrediting or contradicting the definition of the situation that is being maintained. The mythology of the team will dwell upon these disruptive events. We find that performers, audience, and outsiders all utilize techniques for saving the show, whether by avoiding likely disruptions or by correcting for unavoided ones, or by making it possible for others to do so. To ensure that these techniques will be employed, the team will tend to select members who are loyal, disciplined, and circumspect, and to select an audience that is tactful.

The Anthropomorphic Model of Man

In their book entitled *The Explanation of Social Behaviour*, Harré and Secord (1972: 84) place Goffman's work in a larger frame that they hope will provide a "paradigm shift" in the analysis of social interaction. The basic principle in their anthropomorphic model of man is that for scientific purposes one should treat people as if they were human beings. That is, one should take note of the fact that the use of language is what distinguishes human beings from other creatures. The language is used to monitor self behavior. Thus an understanding of the rules of language helps understand the other rules that are followed in the coordination of social behavior.[3] Like Goffman, Harré and Secord (1972: 147) observe that "in social situations people present themselves under what they take to be suitable personas."

The natural unit of social activity is the "episode" during which the participants follow a plan or carry out a sequence of actions necessary to complete a task. The beginning and end of an episode is often marked by a ceremony (Harré and Secord, 1972: 149-153, 176-204). Three types of episodes are identified: (1) formal episodes, that can be either liturgical or games, in which there are rules for what should be done, when, and by whom, (2) routines, such as servicing a car where the actions follow a natural sequence of events, and (3) entertainments, where there is neither "upshot nor outcome" from the actions performed. Formal episodes can in turn be classified according to eight types derived from three dichotomies: genuine-simulated, ceremonial-causal, and cooperative-competitive. For the analysis of social behavior from a dramaturgical standpoint, Harré and Secord (1972: 205-206) suggest that one "1. Treat each episode one is engaged in, whether as actor or audience, as a dramatic performance. 2. Reconstruct the script, the stage directions, etc. which can be analyzed according to role-rule model scheme, as if it were a play script in which rituals, games, routines and entertainments were simulated."

An example of the application of this approach appears in *The Rules of Disorder* by Marsh, Rosser, and Harré (1978). Both distant and participant observation plus interviews that are used to record events in British schools and at football (soccer) games reveal order in apparent disorder as people sit in the same places, are aware of what should and should not be done, and have patterns to their chants and rowdiness. A time line, divided into episodes, is used to compare the activities of football fans that occur during the day when there is a home game and when there is an away game (1978: 85). Recognized roles that are played by fans before, during, or after a match are those of chant leader, aggro leader, nutter, hooligan, organizer, fighter, and heavy drinker (1978: 66-82).

Harré's (1979) most systematic presentation of his dramaturgical approach is given in his book: *Social Being : A Theory for Social Psychology.* Still following Goffman's lead, he believes that "the pursuit of reputation in the eyes of others is the overriding preoccupation of human life" (1979: 3). In public and collective life, there is an interplay between a practical order concerned with production of the means of life, and an expressive order concerned with honor and reputation. In other words, social interaction has both task and social-emotional aspects. Although Harré begins his presentation with the emphasis on honor and reputation (or aspects of "L" in terms of functional analysis), before he is finished he has considered the importance of factors of distribution and production ("A" in functional terms) and power ("G" in functional terms). Factors related to the functional area of "I" such as interpersonal liking or group solidarity are not emphasized.

For the task side of social interaction, Harré suggests a problem-solving model that is based on "accounts" of the ways in which people solve the problems that come from their physical or social environment (1979: 167 ff.). For the social-emotional side he recommends the dramaturgical model that involves Harré (1979: 159):

(1) scene—a product of setting and situation.
(2) action—scenarios classified as remedies (to restore dignity), resolutions (to ratify relationships), or monodramas (when speaking as if

other voices were speaking or commenting on self); all other scenarios are dominated by the practical.

(3)   actor—a person psychologically distinct from, but publicly immersed in, a part.

In his chapter on social action as drama, Harré brings together many of the concepts in the dramaturgical approach that follow from or elaborate on Goffman's perspective. One additional role is described that could be included in the list of basic roles given in Chapter 1. This is the role of *critic,* who provides informed commentary upon action, players, scene, and scenario (1979: 192). He notes that social scientists, like himself, alternate between the roles of producers, audience members, and critics.

Phases in the Development of Social Dramas

As an anthropologist observing the Ndembu people of Zambia, Victor Turner (1974: 33-43) concluded that one of the most arresting properties of village life was the propensity towards conflict. Conflict was rife in the groups of two dozen or so kinsfolk who made up a village community. It manifested itself in public episodes of tension eruption that Turner called "social dramas." Not every social drama reached a clear resolution, but enough did for Turner to identify the "processional form" of the drama. There were four main phases:

(1)   *Breach* of regular, norm-governed, social relations occurs between persons or groups. There is always something altruistic about the symbolic breach. Although the breach may be made by an individual, he always acts, or believes he acts, on behalf of other parties, whether they are aware of it or not.

(2)   Following the breach, a phase of mounting *crisis* supervenes, during which, unless the breach can be sealed off quickly, there is a tendency for the breach to widen and extend until it becomes coextensive with some dominant cleavage in the widest set of relevant social relations to which the conflicting or antagonistic parties belong.

(3)   The third phase is *redressive action* when "mechanisms" informal or formal, institutionalized or ad hoc, are swiftly brought into operation by leading or structurally representative members of the disturbed social system. These mechanisms vary in type and complexity with such factors as: the depth and shared social significance of the breach, the social inclusiveness of the crisis, the nature of the social group within which the breach took place, the degree of autonomy with reference to wider or external systems of social

relations. They may range from personal advice and informal mediation or arbitration to formal juridical and legal machinery, and—to resolve certain kinds of crisis or to legitimate other modes of resolution—to the performance of public ritual.

When redress fails, there is usually regression to crisis. At this point direct force may be used, in the varied forms of war, revolution, intermittent acts of violence, repression, or rebellion. Where the disturbed community is small and relatively weak, vis-à-vis the central authority, regression to crisis tends to become a matter of endemic, pervasive, smoldering factionalism, without sharp, overt confrontations between consistently distinct parties.

(4)   The final phase consists either of the *reintegration* of the disturbed social group or of the social recognition and legitimization of irreparable schism between the contesting parties. After the fourth phase, it is quite likely that the social structure will have changed in noticeable ways.[4]

Notes

1. Comments on Burke's approach are given by Duncan (1968, 1969) and Overington (1977).

2. Comments on Goffman's work are given by Messinger, Sampson, and Towne (1962), Ditton (1980), and Wilshire (198 2: 274-281).

3. Perinbanayagam (1982: 118) provides considerable detail concerning the influence of the structure of language on the development of the self image. In his description of the customs of Jaffna, a part of the island of Sri Lanka inhabited by Tamil-speaking Hindus, he also describes the structure of religion, myths, and astrology and the ways in which they influence the self conception. The people of Jaffna view the world as essentially a theater in which people play out their parts. Astrologers help an individual construct a "myth of the self" that serves as a personal guide for action.

4. In a review of research on gatherings, demonstrations, and riots, McPhail and Wohlstein (1983) report that they could find no studies of phase movement during the previous 15 years of research on protests. Rather there was a focus on the presence or absence of single variables such as milling, queueing, police control, emotion, violence, looting, and sniping. They may have overlooked the study by Feagin and Hahn (1973) that reports four stages that typically occurred in Ghetto riots in the United States and the study of Wright (1978) that reports four phases in looting.

Appendix 2

Functional Analysis of Smelser's Phase Movement in Collective Behavior[1]

Smelser's (1962) functional analysis of various types of collective behavior, many of which involve conflict, provides a rich source of hypotheses concerning the development of these types of behavior around themes and plots. Smelser's ideas are especially relevant when one considers the content of interaction in terms of the AGIL categories as defined in Chapter 1 of this volume.

A tour through Smelser's (1962) *Theory of Collective Behavior* is similar to an archeological expedition at a site already partly worked by another team. Through his application of functional analysis, Smelser has revealed many of the connections between different types of collective behavior. But his excavations have not been uniform. In some places, he stops short of revealing the latent structure. In others, he has failed to distinguish materials from several layers so that aspects of different structures have been grafted together as if they were part of the same whole. In this appendix, I will first review some of the major parts of Smelser's theory to highlight his basic scheme, and then go on to show how the scheme can be extended to form a hypothesis about the phases in group development that is implicit in the theory.

Collective behavior is conceptualized by Smelser as "value-added" process where there is a necessary condition at each stage for the appropriate and effective addition of value at the next stage (1962: 14). He goes to some length to explain that there may be no empirical uniformities in the sequence of stages because an event or situation may be in existence before it is actually activated. However, the order in which he lists the determinants of collective behavior does suggest an order that we might expect to appear most of the time. The determinants are as follows:

(1) Structural conduciveness
(2) Structural strain
(3) Growth and spread of a generalized belief
(4) Precipitating factors
(5) Mobilization of participants for action
(6) The operation of social control

Next Smelser introduces the cybernetic hierarchy of control in which units that are high on information control those that are high on energy. He refers to the hierarchy of the four functional areas as: values, norms, mobilization into organized roles, and situational facilities. These areas are labeled in Table A2.1 as L,I,G, and A to stand for the Parsonian designations of: latent pattern-maintenance and tension management, integration, goal-attainment, and adaptation.

The cybernetic hierarchy is used to order the components of social action along two dimensions. Table A2.1 reproduces Smelser's basic paradigm (1962: 44). It is clear in the table that the cybernetic hierarchy runs across from left to right in the order L,I,G, and A. It is also clear that the hierarchy runs from top to bottom. However the fit between the four AGIL categories and the seven levels of specificity is not clearly stated. Smelser gives a hint in a footnote on page 37 where he tells us that "Levels 2, 3, and 4 parallel Levels 5, 6, and 7, respectively." But the levels are not labeled directly. Given the content at the various levels that Smelser elaborates in the text, it is probable that he would label the levels: L,I,G,A,I,G,A, with the top four levels at the social system level and levels 5-7 at the organization or institutional level. But Level 4 also has characteristics of L as it refers to "legitimization of individual commitment" under *values* and "specification of requirements for individual observation of norms" under *norms*. The entry for *mobilization* (G) is "transition to adult-role assumption." This is probably our best clue. Level 4 seems to include elements

TABLE A2.1 Levels of Specificity of the Components of Social Action

Level		Values L	Norms I	Mobilization of Motivation for Organized Action G	Situational Facilities A
L	1	Societal values	General conformity	Socialized motivation	Preconceptions concerning causality
I	2	Legitimization of values for institutionalized sectors	Specification of norms according to institutional sectors	Generalized performance capacity	Codification of knowledge
G	3	Legitimization of rewards	Specification of norms according to types of roles and organizations	Trained capacity	Technology, or specification of knowledge in situational terms
A L	4	Legitimization of individual commitment	Specification of requirements for individual observation of norms	Transition to adult-role assumption	Procurement of wealth, power, or prestige to activate Level 3
I	5	Legitimization of competing values	Specification of norms of competing institutional sectors	Allocation to sector of society	Allocation of effective technology to sector of society
G	6	Legitimization of values for realizing organizational roles	Specification of rules of cooperation and coordination within organization	Allocation to specific roles or organizations	Allocation of effective technology to roles or organization
A	7	Legitimization of values for expenditure of effort	Specification of schedules and programs to regulate activity	Allocation to roles and tasks within organization	Allocation of facilities within organization to attain concrete goals

More Specific

More Specific

of both L and A. It represents the lowest level of the social system and the highest level of individual involvement in an organization.

By clarifying the fact that the seven levels represent two overlapping sequences of LIGA - LIGA, we note another inconsistency in the table. The first three levels under *mobilization* (G) refer to the socialization of the individual, where "Level 4, then, corresponds roughly to adolescence in the individual's life, when he moves into the adult realm of more responsible motivational commitment to role" (Smelser, 1962: 40). Thus the first three levels of L,I, and A represent the social system level, and the levels under G represent the individual level. Further, current usage of the AGIL categories suggests that if the process of socialization is to be included in the paradigm, it would appear as part of "L" because it involves bringing new units into the system and defining the "meaning of all this" for them.

At various points in the text, it is helpful to keep in mind the correspondence between the seven levels of specificity and the AGIL hierarchy. For example, in the discussion of *strain* (1962: 51ff.), the kind of strain associated with A is *ambiguity* with G is *power distribution*, with I is *role conflict*, and with L is *legitimacy*. Although Smelser (1962: 49) proposes that "any kind of strain may be a determinant of any kind of collective behavior," the type of strain would seem to focus the problem in one of the functional areas and thus contribute to the overall definition of the situation. An example from the United States during the Civil Rights Movement illustrates the relationship between the perceived source of strain and the form of collective behavior. When Martin Luther King led the march on Washington "for Peace and Freedom," the problem of the American black person was seen as primarily legal (I sector). If only the law could be changed to restore civil rights, then it was hoped that the problem would be solved. But once blacks were free to sit at any lunch counter, they found that they did not have the money to buy a hamburger. So the next year in the "Poor People's March" the focus was on the economic sector (A). But the distribution of resources in turn seemed to be controlled by the political system. So the next summer, the "Mississippi Summer," the focus shifted to voter registration in the South. But the "Old Negro" was not confident enough to participate in politics. A new image, of a "New Negro" was needed. That summer the phrase "Black Power" was used, and later "Black is Beautiful." The new emphasis on black identity (L) turned out to be the key to change. Once blacks had gone back to "square one" to develop an entirely new definition of the situation at the top of the cybernetic hierarchy, the other changes followed more easily.

Once a set of persons locate a source of strain in one of the cells in Table A2-1, Smelser suggests that they form a *generalized belief* that the problem can be overcome if something is changed either upward or to the left (or both) in the table. Thus hysteria—which Smelser (1962: 83-84) defines as A—leads to panic, wish fulfillment (A) to craze, hostility (G) to scapegoating or mob violence, a norm oriented belief (I) to a reform movement, and a value-oriented belief (L) to political and religious revolution, nationalist movements, secessions, and formation of cults. Because hysteria and panic are more individual behavior than collective behavior, I would suggest treating them at a lower system level, of the individual in a social situation, leaving wish fulfillment and the craze as the lowest order of actual *collective* behavior.

There are a number of other points in Smelser's presentation of the theory of collective behavior where the additional step of coding his lists according to AGIL will reveal areas that have been omitted or suggest linkages between hypotheses that may not readily be apparent. As an example, one can note a set of stages that seem implicit in the theory in the development of one of the instances of collective behavior described by Smelser. Perhaps the clearest picture of the stages in development are given in Smelser's (1962: 134, Figure 6) diagram of the value-added process for a panic. Along an arrow pointing from left to right he gives the stages as:

Structural Conduciveness	Strain	Anxiety	Precipitating Factor	Hysteria	Mobilization
(L)	(L)	(A)	(I)	(I)	(G)

Below each stage, I have added a code in terms of AGIL. The stages appear to follow an order that is apparent in various types of learning groups (see Chapter 1 of this volume). First, the basic purpose of the activity is defined (L); second, resources are gathered or new skills acquired (A); third, the group is reorganized and roles are differentiated (I); and fourth, the members work at the task (G). Finally there is a terminal phase in which the group returns to L to redefine the relationships between the members and the group is disbanded. In Smelser's theory, both structural conduciveness and strain can be classified as L because they determine the general type of collective behavior. The next stage involves anxiety, which Smelser has identified as a concern about resources (A). The precipitating factor and the emotion that follows (in the case of panic the emotion is hysteria) seem to determine the size of the group or groups that will be involved and the nature of the leadership required, thus forming the I stage. Finally, the stage of mobilization is the enactment of the event (G).

Note

1. This analysis was presented as a paper at the meeting of the Association for Sociologists in Southern Africa, Kwaluseni, Swaziland, June 1975.

Appendix 3

Four-Dimensional Analysis of Polti's 36 Dramatic Situations

This appendix supplements the description of the four-dimensional analysis of Polti's (1977) 36 dramatic situations given in Chapter 2. Some examples are provided for each of the seven sets of situations that were identified.

My procedure was first to depict the roles and objects described by Polti in each of the 36 situations on a field diagram similar to that suggested by Bales and Cohen (see Chapter 1) using the four dimensions of interaction. I then sorted the field diagrams into sets of diagrams according to system level and the major interaction dimension that seemed to be dominant. The result was to reveal seven sets, four at the social system level where the focus is on the interplay of several characters, and three at the personality level. The difference in system levels is recognized by Polti (1977: 67) in his description of various types of individual self-sacrifice, which he groups together with the observation that "the field of conflict is no longer the visible world, but the soul." Polti also recognizes two other sets of situations that are similar to two other types derived from the four-dimensional analysis. Thus, although Polti distinguishes 36 types, he also recognizes some similarities among sets of them. The sets appear below with a listing of the numbers of Polti's types that are included in each set and two examples of the types.

A. *Social System Level*

(1) A hero (upward, positive, serious) as protagonist, a villain (upward, negative, serious) as antagonist, and a third party or object. Conformity or anticonformity is not a major issue. There are 9 situations in this set (numbers 1,2,3,4,5,8,9,12,30).

> *Examples:* #2—Deliverance: the rescue of a condemned person where the cast includes an unfortunate, a threatener, and a rescuer.
>
> #9—Daring enterprise: preparations for war or expeditions where the cast includes a bold leader, an object, and an adversary.

(2) The emphasis is on the relative power of the protagonist (downward) and the antagonist (upward). There are 6 situations in this set (Numbers 6,7,10,24,31,36).

> *Examples:* #6—Disaster: a great reversal of roles when a defeat is suffered or there is a natural catastrophe. The cast includes a vanquished power and a victorious enemy or messenger.
>
> #31—Conflict with a god: a struggle against or controversy with a deity. The cast includes a mortal and an immortal.

(3) The emphasis is on the positive-negative dimension of social interaction. Persons who should like each other do not. Also as Newcomb (1953) has observed, problems occur when a person likes another person who does not also like a third person or object. The situations of this type generally involve a triangular relationship where there is an imbalance of this sort. There are 7 situations in this set (Numbers 13,14,18,28,29,32,33).

> *Examples:* #13—Emnity of kinsmen: hatred between persons such as brothers or father and son who would be expected to love each other. The cast includes a malevolent kinsman, and a hated or reciprocally hating kinsman.
>
> #29—An enemy loved: a loved one is hated by a kinsman of the lover. The lover is the slayer of the father, brother, and so on, of his or her beloved. The cast includes the beloved enemy, the lover, and the hater.

(4) The emphasis is on the conforming-nonconforming dimension of social interaction. Although the crime could be of any type, a family member or loved one is usually involved, and in four of the six types, the crime

is either adultery or incest. There are 6 situations in this set (Numbers 15,19,25,26,27,34).

> *Examples:* #15—Murderous adulterer: the slaying of a husband or wife by or for a paramour. The cast includes two adulterers and a betrayed husband or wife.
>
> #34—Remorse: remorse for an unknown crime, murder, or adultery. The cast includes the culprit, the victim or the sin, and the interrogator.

B. *Individual or Personality Level*

(1) The fatal flaw: the upward, positive, serious ideal self of the protagonist is contrasted with his or her upward negative behavior. This is similar to Set 1 at the social system level but the struggle is between two aspects of the same person. There are 2 situations in this set (Numbers 16, 17).

> *Examples:* #16—Madness: a kinsman or a lover is slain in madness. Cast includes a madman and a victim.
>
> #17—Fatal imprudence: the imprudence or curiosity of the protagonist causes his own misfortune. The cast includes the imprudent and the victim or object lost.

(2) Search: the theme emphasizes the upward-downward dimension because the relatively powerless protagonist searches for someone overcoming obstacles. There are 2 situations in this set (Numbers 11, 35).

> *Examples:* #11—Enigma: a search for a person who must be found (or a riddle to be solved) on pain of death. The cast includes the interrogator, the seeker, and the problem.
>
> #35—Recovery of a lost one: often this is a double recovery where the scene ends with the exclamations "my daughter . . . my mother." The cast includes the seeker and the one found.

(3) Self sacrifice: The theme is of conformity to the ideal self versus some pragmatic action. There are 4 situations in this set (Numbers 20,21,22,23).

> *Examples:* #20—Self-sacrificing for an ideal: sacrifice of life for the sake of one's word, success of one's people, faith, king, cause, and so on. The cast includes the hero, the ideal, the "creditor" or the person or the thing sacrificed.
>
> #22—All sacrificed for a passion: Religious vows of chastity are broken for a passion or a future is ruined. The cast includes the lover, the object of the fatal passion, and the person or thing sacrificed.

We note that at the individual level, three of the four themes that appeared at the social system level are also evident (hero-villain, upward-downward, and conformity-nonconformity). However there is no theme of positive-negative balance for the individual. At both levels the serious-expressive dimensions appear to be absent as a main focus of the drama. This is because Polti has chosen to classify situations without regard to whether or not the intent was to be serious or expressive. Any one of these situations could appear in a drama that was serious (tragedy or melodrama) or expressive (comedy and farce). However Polti notes, as did Bentley, that situations built upon love, especially incest and adultery, are more likely to appear in comedy and farce.

Bibliography

Allen, Vernon L., and Karl E. Scheibe (eds.) 1982 The Social Context of Conduct: Psychological Writings of Theodore Sarbin. New York: Praeger.

Aram, M. 1977 "Peace in Nagaland," pp. 208-219 in A. P. Hare and H. H. Blumberg (eds.) Liberation Without Violence. London: Rex Collings.

Argyle, Michael (ed.) 1973 Social Encounters: Readings in Social Interaction. Chicago: Aldine.

Bales, Robert F. 1950 Interaction Process Analysis: A Method for the Study of Small Groups. Cambridge, MA: Addison-Wesley.

——— 1970 Personality and Interpersonal Behavior. New York: Holt, Rinehart, & Winston.

——— 1984 "The integration of social psychology." Social Psychology Quarterly 47 (1): 98-101.

Bales, Robert F., and Stephen P. Cohen, with Stephen A. Williamson 1979 SYMLOG: A System for the Multiple Level Observation of Groups. New York: Free Press.

Benedetti, Robert L. 1976 Seeming, Being and Becoming: Acting in Our Century. New York: Drama Book Specialists.

Bentley, Eric 1967 The Life of the Drama. New York: Atheneum.

Berger, Peter L., and Thomas Luckman 1967 The Social Construction of Reality: A Treatise in the Sociology of Knowledge. Garden City, NY: Doubleday.

Berne, Eric 1964 Games People Play: The Psychology of Human Relationships. New York: Grove Press.

Bion, W. R. 1961 Experiences in Groups and Other Papers. New York: Basic Books.

Blau, Peter M. 1968 "Social exchange," pp. 452-458 in D. L. Sills (ed.) International Encyclopedia of the Social Sciences, vol. 7. New York: Macmillan.

Boulding, Kenneth 1956 The Image. Ann Arbor: University of Michigan Press.

Brissett, Dennis, and Charles Edgely (eds.) 1975 Life as Theater: A Dramaturgical Sourcebook. Chicago: Aldine.

Brockett, Oscar G. 1964 The Theatre: An Introduction. New York: Holt, Rinehart, & Winston.

Brook, Peter 1968 The Empty Space. London: MacGibbon & Kee.

Brzezinski, Zbigniew 1983 Power and Principle. New York: Farrar, Straus, & Giroux.

Buber, Martin 1970 I and Thou. New York: Scribner.

Burke, Kenneth 1945 A Grammar of Motives. New York: Prentice Hall.

——— 1968 "Dramatism," pp. 445-452 in D. L. Sills (ed.) International Encyclopedia of the Social Sciences, vol. 7. New York: Macmillan.

Burns, Elizabeth 1972 Theatricality: A Study of Convention in the Theatre and in Social Life. New York: Harper Torchbooks.
Burton, John 1979 Deviance, Terrorism, and War: The Process of Solving Unsolved Social and Political Problems. Oxford: Martin Robertson.
Carter, Jimmy 1982 Keeping Faith. New York: Bantam Books.
Caws, Peter 1979 Sartre. London: Routledge & Kegan Paul.
Clark, Brian 1971 Group Theatre. London: Pitman.
Clay, James H., and Daniel Krempel 1967 The Theatrical Image. New York: McGraw-Hill.
Clutterbuck, Richard 1973 Protest and the Urban Guerrilla. London: Cassell.
Cole, David 1975 The Theatrical Event: A Mythos, A Vocabulary, A Perspective. Middletown, CT: Wesleyan University Press.
Cooley, Charles H. 1902 Human Nature and the Social Order. New York: Scribner.
Dayan, Moshe 1981 Breakthrough: A Personal Account of the Egypt-Israel Peace Negotiations. London: Weidenfeld & Nicholson.
Desai, Narayan 1972 Towards a Non-violent Revolution. Rajghat, Varanasi, India: Sarva Seva Sangh Prakashan.
Deutsch, Morton 1973 The Resolution of Conflict: Constructive and Destructive Processes. New Haven, CT: Yale University Press.
Ditton, Jason (ed.) 1980 The View from Goffman. New York: St. Martin's Press.
Dodd, Stuart C., and Stefan C. Christopher 1969 "How to produce consensus: A progress report from project consensus." Journal of Human Relations 17(4): 628-629.
Duncan, Hugh D. 1968 Symbols in Society. New York: Oxford University Press.
——— 1969 Symbols and Social Theory. New York: Oxford University Press.
Edelman, Murray 1977 The Symbolic Uses of Politics. Urbana, IL: University of Illinois Press.
Effrat, Andrew 1968 "Editor's introduction." Sociological Inquiry 38(2): 97-103.
——— 1976 "Introduction," pp. 662-680 in J. J. Loubser, R. C. Baum, A. Effrat, and V. M. Lidz (eds.) Explorations in General Theory in Social Science. New York: Free Press.
Eilts, Herman 1980 "Saving Camp David: Improve the framework." Foreign Policy (Fall): 3-20.
Feagin, Joe R., and Harlan Hahn 1973 Ghetto Revolts: The Politics of Violence in American Cities. New York: Macmillan.
Fisher, Roger, and William Ury 1978 International Mediation: A Working Guide: Ideas for the Practitioner. New York: International Peace Academy.
Follett, Mary Parker 1924 Creative Experience. New York: Longmans, Green.
Fry, Christopher 1962 "Comedy," pp. 67-70 in S. Barnet, M. Berman, and W. Burto (eds.) Aspects of the Drama: A Handbook. Boston: Little, Brown.
Goffman, Erving 1959 The Presentation of Self in Everyday Life. Garden City, NY: Doubleday.
——— 1961 Encounters: Two Studies in the Sociology of Interaction. Indianapolis: Bobbs-Merrill.
——— 1963 Behavior in Public Places: Notes on the Social Organization of Gatherings. New York: Free Press.
——— 1967 Interaction Ritual: Essays in Face-to-face Behavior. Chicago: Aldine.
——— 1968 Asylums: Essays on the Social Situation of Mental Patients and Other Inmates. Harmonsworth, Middlesex, England: Penguin Books.

———— 1970 Strategic Interaction. Oxford: Basil Blackwell.

———— 1972 Relations in Public: Microstudies of Public Order. New York: Harper & Row.

———— 1974 Frame Analysis: An Essay on the Organization of Experience. New York: Harper & Row.

Hall, Jay, and W. H. Watson 1970 "The effects of normative intervention on group decision-making performance." Human Relations 23(4): 299-317.

Hamilton, Clayton 1939 The Theory of the Theatre: And Other Principles of Dramatic Criticism. New York: Holt, Rinehart, & Winston.

Hammond-Tooke, William D. 1975 Command or Consensus: The Development of the Transkeian Local Government. Cape Town: David Philip.

Hare, A. Paul 1976 Handbook of Small Group Research (Second edition). New York: Free Press.

———— 1977 "Applying the third party approach," pp. 265-287 in A. P. Hare and H. H. Blumberg (eds.) Liberation Without Violence. London: Rex Collings.

———— 1980 "A dramaturgical analysis of street demonstrations: Washington, D.C., 1971 and Cape Town, 1976." Group Psychotherapy, Psychodrama and Sociometry 33: 92-120.

———— 1982 Creativity in Small Groups. Beverly Hills, CA: Sage.

———— 1983a "A functional interpretation of interaction," pp. 429-447 in H. H. Blumberg, A. P. Hare, V. Kent, and M. Davies (eds.) Small Groups and Social Interaction, vol. 2. Chichester, England: John Wiley.

Hare, A. Paul (ed.) 1983b The Struggle for Democracy in South Africa: Conflict and Conflict Resolution. Cape Town, South Africa: Centre for Intergroup Studies, University of Cape Town.

———— 1984 Cyprus Resettlement Project: An Instance of International Peace-making. Beer Sheva, Israel: Department of Behavioral Sciences, Ben-Gurion University of the Negev.

Hare, A. Paul, and Herbert H. Blumberg (eds.) 1968 Nonviolent Direct Action: American Cases: Social-Psychological Analyses. Washington, DC: Corpus Books.

———— 1977 Liberation Without Violence: A Third Party Approach. London: Rex Collings.

———— 1980 A Search for Peace and Justice: Reflections of Michael Scott. London: Rex Collings.

Hare, A. Paul, and David Naveh 1984 "Group development at Camp David Summit, 1978." Small Group Behavior 15 (3): 299-318.

———— 1985 "Creative problem solving: Camp David Summit, 1978." Small Group Behavior 16.

Hare, A. Paul, and Max H. von Broembsen 1979 "The use of consensus at the Constitutional Conference in South West Africa." Paper presented at meeting of the Association for Sociology in Southern Africa, Maseru, Lesotho, June.

Hare, A. Paul, and Ellen Wilkinson 1977 "Cyprus: Conflict and its resolution," pp. 239-247 in A. P. Hare and H. H. Blumberg (eds.) Liberation Without Violence. London: Rex Collings.

Harré, Rom 1979 Social Being: A Theory for Social Psychology. Oxford: Basil Blackwell.

Harré, Rom, and Paul F. Secord 1972 The Explanation of Social Behaviour. Oxford: Basil Blackwell.

Hodgson, John, and Ernest Richards 1974 Improvisation (Revised edition). London: Eyre Methuen.

Horner, Dudley, and Alida Kooy 1980 Conflict on South Africa Mines: 1972-1979. Cape Town: South African Labour and Development Research Unit, University of Cape Town.

Innes, Christopher 1981 Holy Theatre: Ritual and the Avante Garde. Cambridge: Cambridge University Press.

Janis, Irving L. 1982 Groupthink: Psychological Studies of Policy Decisions and Fiascoes. Boston: Houghton Mifflin.

Johnstone, Keith 1979 Impro: Improvisation and the Theatre. New York: Theatre Arts Books.

Katz, Daniel, and Robert L. Kahn 1978 The Social Psychology of Organizations (Second edition). New York: John Wiley.

Klapp, Orrin E. 1962 Heroes, Villains, and Fools: The Changing American Character. Englewood Cliffs, NJ: Prentice-Hall.

Ladlau, L. K. 1975 The Cato Manor Riots. Unpublished Master's Thesis, Department of History, University of Natal, South Africa.

Lahr, John, and Jonathan Price 1973 Life-Show: How to See Theater in Life and Life in Theater. New York: Viking Press.

Leary, Timothy 1957 Interpersonal Diagnosis of Personality. New York: Ronald.

Lewin, Kurt 1935 A Dynamic Theory of Personality. New York: McGraw-Hill.

Lofland, John 1981 "Collective behavior: The elementary forms," pp.411-446 in M. Rosenberg and R. H. Turner (eds.) Social Psychology: Sociological Perspectives. New York: Basic Books.

Lyman, Stanford M., and Marvin B. Scott 1970 A Sociology of the Absurd. New York: Appleton-Centry-Crofts.

——— 1975 The Drama of Social Reality. New York: Oxford University Press.

MacCannell, Dean 1973 Nonviolent Action as Theater: A Dramaturgical Analysis of 146 Demonstrations. Haverford, PA: Haverford College, Nonviolent Action Research Project, Monograph No. 10.

McArthur, David J. 1982 "Computer vision and perceptual psychology." Psychological Bulletin 92 (2): 283-309.

McPhail, Clark, and Ronald T. Wohlstein 1983 "Individual and collective behaviors within gatherings, demonstrations, and riots." Annual Review of Sociology 9: 579-600.

Maines, David R. 1981 "Recent develoment in symbolic interaction," pp. 461-487 in G. P. Stone and H. A. Farberman (eds.) Social Psychology Through Symbolic Interaction (Second edition). New York: John Wiley.

Maree, Johann 1983 "The strike, U.A.W., PEBCO and the Workers' Committee," pp. 112-123 in A. P. Hare (ed.) The Struggle for Democracy in South Africa. Cape Town: Centre for Intergroup Studies, University of Cape Town.

Marsh, Peter, Elizabeth Rosser, and Rom Harré 1978 The Rules of Disorder. London: Routledge & Kegan Paul.

Mead, George H. 1934 Mind, Self and Society. Chicago: University of Chicago Press.

Messinger, Sheldon L., with Harold Sampson and Robert D. Towne 1962 "Life as theater: Some notes on the dramaturgic approach to social reality." Sociometry 25: 98-110.

Miles-Brown, John 1980 Directing Drama. London: Peter Owen.

Moreno, Jacob L. 1947 The Theatre of Spontaneity. Beacon, NY: Beacon House.

——— 1953 Who Shall Survive? (Revised edition) Beacon, NY: Beacon House.

——— 1972 Psychodrama, First Volume (Fourth edition). Beacon, NY: Beacon House.

Moreno, Jacob L., in collaboration with Zerka T.Moreno 1969 Psychodrama: Third Volume, Action Therapy and Principles of Practice. Beacon, NY: Beacon House.

Naveh, David, and A. Paul Hare forthcoming "Staging and conflict resolution: Camp David 1978."

Neisser, Ulric 1976 Cognition and Reality: Principles and Implications of Cognitive Psychology. San Francisco: W. H. Freeman.

Nemiroff, Paul M., and Donald C. King 1975 "Group decision-making performance as influenced by consensus and self-orientation." Human Relations 28 (1): 1-21.

Overington, Michael A. 1977 "Kenneth Burke and the method of dramatism." Theory and Society 4 (1): 131-156.

Parsons, Talcott 1961 "An outline of the social system," pp. 30-79 in T. Parsons et al. (eds.) Theories of Society. New York: Free Press.

——— 1968 "Social interaction," pp. 429-441 in D. L. Sills (ed.) International Encyclopedia of the Social Sciences, vol. 7. New York: Macmillan.

Pepper, Stephen C. 1942 World Hypotheses. Berkeley: University of California Press.

Perinbanayagam, R. S. 1982 The Karmic Theater: Self, Society, and Astrology in Jaffna. Amherst: University of Massachusetts Press.

Polti, Georges 1977 The Thirty-Six Dramatic Situations. Boston: Writer.

Raven, Bertram H., and Jeffrey Z. Rubin 1983 Social Psychology (Second edition). New York: John Wiley.

Redl, Fritz 1965 "Group emotion and leadership," pp. 71-87 in A. P. Hare, E. F. Borgatta, and R. F. Bales (eds.) Small Groups: Studies in Social Interaction (Revised edition). New York: Knopf.

Rothman, Rozann 1981 "Political symbolism," pp. 285-340 in S. L. Long (ed.) the Handbook of Political Behavior, vol. 2. New York: Plenum Press.

Schapera, Isaac 1962 "Political institutions," pp. 173-195 in I. Schapera (ed.) The Bantu-speaking Tribes of South Africa. Cape Town: Maskew Miller.

Schechner, Richard 1973 Environmental Theater. New York: Hawthorn Books.

Scheff, Thomas J. 1967 "Toward a sociological model of consensus." American Sociological Review 23 (1): 32-45.

Smelser, Neil J. 1962 Theory of Collective Behavior. New York: Free Press.

Smith, A.C.H. 1975 Orghast at Persepolis. London: Eyre Methuen.

Sobel, Bernard (ed.) 1959 The New Theatre Handbook: and Digest of Plays. New York: Crown.

Spolin, Viola 1977 Improvisation for the Theatre: A Handbook of Teaching and Directing Techniques. London: Pitman.

Stanislavski, Constantin 1961 Creating a Role. New York: Theatre Arts.
Stock, Dorothy, and Herbert H. Thelen 1958 Emotional Dynamics and Group Culture. New York: New York University Press.
Stone, Gregory P., and Harvey A. Farberman (eds.) 1981 Social Psychology Through Symbolic Interaction (Second edition). New York: John Wiley.
Stryker, Sheldon 1981 "Symbolic interactionism: Themes and variations," pp. 3-29 in M. Rosenberg and R. H. Turner (eds.) Social Psychology: Sociological Perspectives. New York: Basic Books.
Swanson, Guy E. 1968 "Symbolic interaction," pp. 441-445 in D. L. Sills (ed.) International Encyclopedia of the Social Sciences, vol. 7. New York: Macmillan.
Taylor, Irving A. 1975 "An emerging view of creative actions," pp. 297-325 in I. A. Taylor and J. W. Getzels (eds.) Perspectives in Creativity. Chicago: Aldine.
Thoreau, Henry David 1949 Walden. New York: Signet.
Turner, Victor 1974 Dramas, Fields, and Metaphors: Symbolic Action in Human Society. Ithaca: Cornell University Press.
Vance, Cyrus R. 1983 Hard Choices: Four Critical Years in America's Foreign Policy. New York: Simon and Schuster.
Van Laan, Thomas F. 1970 The Idiom of Drama. Ithaca: Cornell University Press.
Volkart, Edmund H. (ed.) 1951 Social Behavior and Personality: Contributions of W. I. Thomas to Theory and Social Research. New York: Social Science Research Council.
Wagner, Betty J. 1979 Dorothy Heathcote: Drama as a Learning Medium. London: Hutchinson.
Walker, Charles C. 1977 "Nonviolence in Eastern Africa 1962-4," pp. 157-177 in A. P. Hare and H. H. Blumberg (eds.) Liberation Without Violence. London: Rex Collings.
Weizman, Ezer 1981 The Battle for Peace. New York: Bantam Books.
Wessels, P. J. 1960 Report of the Commission Appointed to Investigate and Report on the Occurences in the Districts of Vereeniging (Namely at Sharpeville Location and Evaton) and Vanderbijlpark, Province of the Transvaal, on the 21st of March, 1960.
Wilshire, Bruce 1982 Role Playing and Identity: The Limits of Theatre as Metaphor. Bloomington: Indiana University Press.
Winston, Patrick H. 1977 Artificial intelligence. Reading, MA: Addison-Wesley.
Wish, Myron, and Susan J. Kaplan 1977 "Toward an implicit theory of interpersonal communication." Sociometry 40 (3): 234-246.
Wright, Sam 1978 Crowds and Riots: A Study in Social Organization. London: Sage.
Zurcher, Louis A., and David A. Snow 1981 "Collective behavior: Social movements," pp. 447-482 in M. Rosenberg and R. H. Turner (eds.) Social Psychology: Sociological Perspectives. New York: Basic Books.

Author Index

177

Subject Index

About the Author

A. Paul Hare is currently Professor of Sociology at Ben-Gurion University of the Negev. Previously he taught at Harvard, Haverford, and the University of Cape Town, with associations of one year or less with other universities in the United States, Philippines, Nigeria, Uganda, Rhodesia, Austria, and Israel. Born in 1923 in Washington, DC, he received academic degrees from Swarthmore, Iowa State (Ames, University of Pennsylvania, and Chicago (Ph.D., 1951). His *Handbook of Small Group Research* is the most extensive review of research on group dynamics, and the readings on *Small Groups* that he co-edited (initially with Borgatta and Bales and currently with Blumberg, Kent, and Davies) have provided basic material in the field through three editions. His most recent work on *Creativity in Small Groups* presents four perspectives for the analysis of social interaction, including the dramaturgical perspective that has been elaborated to provide the central theme for the present volume.

In addition to his writing on the subject of small groups, Paul Hare has edited three volumes of case studies on nonviolent action with Herbert Blumberg. He is also the author of many journal articles, the co-editor or editor of the volumes *South Africa, Cooperation in Education* and *The Struggle for Democracy in South Africa,* and the founder and editor of the journal *Israel Social Science Research.*